T0372320

How to Build, Buy, and Sell a Small Business

Small business owners do not have the time or resources to consult with so-called 'business experts' every time a particular issue comes up. It just takes too long for an 'outsider' to understand their particular business niche. Clearly, legal and accounting issues need professional support. But most ongoing issues have to do with judgement calls, not detailed, technical expertise.

This book covers nontechnical issues, such as 'Am I really suited to be an entrepreneur?' managing salespeople, human resources, bribery/corruption, grow or acquire, failing to plan, money management, and selling up on retirement. The book also includes topics such as dealing with cash, potential fraud, bribery, people performance, morales, acquisitions, and much more, including selling your business when the time is right.

The author's approach is to provide practical, experienced advice gleaned over 40 years on the main topics which challenge small business owners every day, not just once or twice a year.

How to Build, Buy, and Sell a Small Business

Essential Tips and Expert Guidance from 40 Years of Small Business Development and Exits

John G. Fisher

Routledge
Taylor & Francis Group

A PRODUCTIVITY PRESS BOOK

Designed cover image: Web Large Image (Public)

First published 2025
by Routledge
605 Third Avenue, New York, NY 10158

and by Routledge
4 Park Square, Milton Park, Abingdon, Oxon, OX14 4RN

Routledge is an imprint of the Taylor & Francis Group, an informa business

Library of Congress Cataloging-in-Publication Data
Names: Fisher, John G., author.
Title: How to buy, build and sell on your small business : essential tips and expert guidance from 40 years of small business development and exits / John G. Fisher.
Description: New York, NY : Routledge, 2025. | Includes bibliographical references and index. | Summary: "Small business owners do not have the time or resources to consult with so-called 'business experts' every time a particular issue comes up. It just takes too long for an 'outsider' to understand their particular business niche. Clearly legal and accounting issues need professional support. But most ongoing issues have to do with judgement calls, not detailed, technical expertise. This book covers non-technical issues such as 'am I really suited to be an entrepreneur?', managing salespeople, human resources, bribery/corruption, grow or acquire, failing to plan, money management and selling up on retirement. The book also includes topics such as: dealing with cash, potential fraud, bribery, people performance, morales, acquisitions and much more including selling your business when the time is right. The authors' approach is to provide practical, experienced advice gleaned over 40 years on the main topics which challenge small business owners every day, not just once or twice a year"—Provided by publisher.
Identifiers: LCCN 2024029304 (print) | LCCN 2024029305 (ebook) |
    ISBN 9781032873374 (hardback) | ISBN 9781032872353 (paperback) |
    ISBN 9781003532118 (ebook)
Subjects: LCSH: Small business—Management. | Success in business.
Classification: LCC HD62.7 .F568 2025 (print) | LCC HD62.7 (ebook) |
    DDC 658.02/2—dc23/eng/20240904
LC record available at https://lccn.loc.gov/2024029304
LC ebook record available at https://lccn.loc.gov/2024029305

ISBN: 978-1-032-87337-4 (hbk)
ISBN: 978-1-032-87235-3 (pbk)
ISBN: 978-1-003-53211-8 (ebk)

DOI: 10.4324/9781003532118

Typeset in Garamond
by Apex CoVantage, LLC

To Carol, without whom no business
would have ever gotten done.

Contents

Acknowledgements

We all stand on the shoulders of giants, so they say, in life as well as in business. Personal success and happiness are built on other people's efforts as well as your own.

With that thought in mind, I need to acknowledge two friends and colleagues from the past without whom none of the buying, selling, and exiting could ever have happened.

Tony Moy was my first real boss, who put me in charge of a business and simply let me get on with it.

Pete Kroeger encouraged, cajoled, and argued my corner with a multitude of finance experts and legal people when I was buying and selling – things I knew very little about when I started out.

With their expert help, the rest became history, and I am enormously grateful to them.

About the Author

John G. Fisher has almost 40 years of experience setting up, building, and selling on small businesses, both for himself and for his clients. As an owner at various times, he has managed an incentive travel business, a motivation agency, an employee engagement consultancy, an app development boutique, and an event software supplier.

During that career, he has also written ten books, spoken at many international conferences, and published a regular column for 20 years for an international meetings and incentives magazine with global reach.

He has devised and run numerous business seminars on such topics as corporate bribery, managing cross-border communication promotions, how channel incentives work, benchmarking, and getting your business ready for sale.

He created the UK's first incentive and motivation online learning course, which became the standard industry diploma for best practice for young people entering the business motivation field.

From his home near Oxford, England, he now runs his own consultancy for anyone wishing to explore how best to sell their small business either to grow faster or as they approach retirement.

email: john@klopartners.co.uk

Introduction

In 1998, I sold my first business for over 5m, much to my surprise. I got half. My business partner had lent me 50,000 to start it up with him and just gave me half the shares. He said I could pay him back when I had the money. I only paid him back the day we jointly sold the business, nine years later. No home loan extension, no bank loans, no family money.

As I studied the legal documents on deal day, I could scarcely believe the sums involved. I had never considered myself an 'entrepreneur' or, indeed, any kind of proper business person. I never studied business or had any business owners in my family. I never asked anyone for business advice. I didn't know any business investors. I didn't read business books. It all just seemed to have happened.

0.1 Or Did It?

True, we did buy another small business, along the way, during the nine years . . . and then sold it again for a small profit. We also acquired a small travel business which simply got absorbed into the main organisation because it never paid its

way as a separate unit. I still did not think I was an entrepreneur or ever identified with the phrase 'small business owner'.
I was just doing my job.

0.2 Becoming an Entrepreneur Gradually

Over the following 30 years, I then set up and sold on four
more businesses – I still have a small stake in a fifth business.
We are hoping to sell it in the next few years.

But it is only now, looking back, that I recognise I really
was an entrepreneur. Throughout most of my career in small
businesses, I appointed myself as the boss and paid myself the
going rate. I thought this was less risky than asking someone
else to do the top job. It was my money, after all. It also meant
I would get paid regularly.

There were lots of things I would have done differently,
given the chance again. But improvements were rarely something I had copied from other people. Stuff I read in trade
magazines, blogs, and websites was often inspiring and entertaining for a short while. But they were rarely helpful to me,
come the beginning of another working week.

0.3 Useful Ideas

This book picks out some useful things I did which other
small business owners may find beneficial to think about.
These are things which changed my way of doing things. Or
simply reminded me that sometimes you just have to act on
instinct rather than agonise about whether 'other owners' do it
this way or not. Or even what the accountant thinks.

My aim is to pass on what I learned, in the hope that other
small business owners do not have to waste time making the
same mistakes as me. Or even worse, waste money trying

things that may well be popular amongst social media business gurus but don't actually work in real life in a small company trying to make its way.

0.4 What's in the Book?

Topics include dealing with cash, potential fraud, bribery, people performance, morale, sales, acquisitions, marketing, legal stuff, monitoring progress, and perhaps most important of all, selling your business, or businesses, when the time is right.

These issues came up time and again over several decades and in almost every business I set up and managed.

So you can just read a chapter or two, or you can read the book from beginning to end – or, indeed, from the end back to the beginning, which might be more instructive!

0.5 SMEs Are Different

One fundamental thing is the fact that SMEs (small- to medium-size enterprises) are not the same as large organisations. Things happen much more quickly, and most employees are not experts or trained in their department speciality, if there are such things in your organisation. You work with what you've got, not with what you wish you had. You have to find your own cash to fund any improvements. Or simply make do and mend.

0.6 Stressful?

Not really. In fact, I found that being in control, or at least feeling I was in control, was much less stressful than working for someone else, especially if you disagree with how they do things. It's also unusual to make yourself redundant.

That said, I did in fact make myself jobless at 63 when I sold the last business I was employed by. I agreed to stay on for the new owners so they could handle the transition for two years. But I decided to quit after 18 months. They didn't know how to get new customers for the business they acquired. It was no longer my job to teach them.

0.7 What Do I Mean by a Small Business?

Probably an enterprise with 30 people or less, but definitely more than 1 person. I may also add, in my opinion, that you should have 'premises' to be a proper small business, whether that is a retail outlet, a warehouse, a factory, or an office of some kind, rather than WFH (working from home). I have a lot of respect for independent contractors, but they are mostly self-employed and rarely manage teams of people. Things are very different once you have an office or employ people or have a physical site to manage.

But the main point is, if I knew back then what I know now, I would have made less mistakes, been a better employer, and retired much earlier. Or made more money. Or even started another business!

If you pick up just one idea that saves you time or money in your SME working life, I would consider this book a success and worth the read.

Chapter 1

Am I Made of the Right Stuff?

Imposter syndrome has been a theme in discussions about public life and big business recently. Have I got what it takes to run a business?

Do I even have the right skills to start up and run a small business? Am I clever enough? Can I learn how to run a business? Will I be strong enough to take risks when the time comes? Will I make any money? Will I survive, financially and mentally?

One of the nagging doubts that will come up throughout your small business career will no doubt be 'ability'. Many young people delay their entry into business life by spending years acquiring technical skills that they think will help them get that all-important first job, so they can then move onwards and upwards in their career.

This is fine in a big organisation. Not much use in a small enterprise.

In particular, the popularity of 'business degrees', or the equivalent of MBAs, seems a must-have for many budding entrepreneurs. In truth, knowing the theory and trying out desk skills are all well and good, if only because you can check if you are on the right track.

But successful entrepreneurs are more likely to simply 'give it a go' and assess the risks as and when they arise. Sales are what matter. Along with cash. Theory is for thinking about later on, if there is ever a reckoning.

Organisations that appear to want these skills from raw recruits are likely to be already long-established. They will have dozens of other experienced employees who can use these skills better or more quickly than you. In truth, you will not be allowed to cause much damage by practising them as a junior. So the risks are very small for the shareholders if it all goes wrong. You don't learn much either, as there are few consequences for any mistakes.

If you are very lucky, say, in the top 1%, you may get a chance years later to impose those disciplines and ideas on others as a senior employee of a large organisation. But a business qualification is unlikely to make you a successful entrepreneur anytime soon. Knowing what other people do or know is not as important as getting it done and learning from experience yourself in a small business environment.

Made from the right stuff? In my early years, I did the marketing for a financial firm. As part of my big company 'training', I went on a 'salesman's course' so I could understand their world. The course was mostly about self-belief and attitude. One saying stood out: *If not now, when? If not me, who?*[1] This phrase echoed in my mind whenever I worried about getting on with things and doing something rather than doing nothing.

1.1 What Is an Entrepreneur?

This leads to the question of what an entrepreneur is.

The business world is full of stories about how famous business personalities sold lemonade outside their home when they were 3 years old. Or invented new game-changing software from their garage in their spare time as a student. Or borrowed/were given some cash from a benevolent aunt and turned it into (even more) millions.

The trouble with these stories is that they are unique. But in no way are they typical examples of early entrepreneurship. They help to backfill a story of an already-famous business person readers want to believe in. Trouble is, if they are not typical, then they are not much help to normal people interested in business as a normal career, having a normal life. What you want to know is, How like me is this story?

Many leading business entrepreneurs are dyslexic. You can be both number dyslexic (dyscalculic) and word dyslexic. This is a huge disadvantage in business as you cannot easily make sense of a table of numbers or a written report. In the case of some leading business people with this disability, it may have worked in their favour. They simply delegated these key tasks to people who did have those skills, then concentrated on other areas, such as salesmanship, market opportunities, and people issues. This is a unique way to be successful, and well done to those who can achieve it. But few people are so naturally talented.

No sane person would recommend that being unable to read a report or make sense of numbers is an essential quality for business success, would they?

Of course, dyslexic people can be successful in many walks of life, particularly in the creative industries. But the odds are stacked against you when developing a small business. Most people, by definition, have average reading and number skills. Not being able to read easily or add up competently is not the ideal basis for a successful entrepreneurial career. You just have to be adequately skilled with enough 'street sense' to ask someone else if you don't know the answer, or perhaps even to understand the question. Lots of financial and legal issues fall into these categories.

1.2 Selling V. Entrepreneurship?

How about that issue of salesmanship? For many members of the public, an *entrepreneur* is someone with the gift of a credible sales patter and being able to spot a sales opportunity where others don't, in almost any situation. This is not being an entrepreneur. This is being good at sales. Often, great salespeople are hopeless at delivery or keeping accurate score. You have to be good at sales. But not so good that you neglect the basic business management skills of delivery, review, and improvement.

Selling is less about product knowledge than about creating empathy. I have been fortunate to work with some truly outstanding salespeople whose main skill was to create empathy within the first 90 seconds of meeting someone new. No amount of training can teach this, or any number of sales techniques from an online course or an enthusiastic life coach.

Entrepreneurship is more about seeing how an idea can be put into practice, preferably for a profit. Of course, salesmanship comes into it. But being the loudest mouth in the room rarely converts into a long-term viable business. People don't warm to megaphones. But they do buy from people they like, even if sometimes what you've got is not exactly what they thought they wanted when they walked through your door.

1.3 What about Coming Up with 'Great Ideas' All the Time?

Another popular idea of entrepreneurship is the ability to generate many ideas to sell services or products. The problem is, most ideas creators are not good at testing them out or learning from mistakes. It takes a different mindset to apply something old to something new and then seeing how it works.

And then keep on doing it until it becomes profitable. It is often said that Edison failed over 1,000 times before his own light bulb 'came on'.

The development of the railways in the 19th century is another entrepreneurial case in point. In a business world dominated by rivers, canals, and a small number of good roads, the idea of creating metal tracks on wooden supports for a vehicle to run along seemed a crazy way to get goods to market. Think of the work to be done setting it up and then making enough 'trains' to pull the goods along. But without this preparatory work, there would have been no Industrial Revolution or mass distribution, on which the modern world economy was built.

It takes an entrepreneur to come up with ways to make that idea possible and keep testing processes until one of them works well enough to get you to the next stage.

When the histories of modern successful organisations are re-told, you often get the impression that an individual had a great idea one day, it worked first time, and millions were made overnight. The truth is far more mundane. A good entrepreneur is more likely to be working in an established industry where the techniques are well-tried and tested. But they are able to see new ways to achieve better results in another market and apply them at a profit. This happens over many years, with many inefficiencies and failures along the way.

You may not consider yourself to be particularly 'creative', measured by, say, the visual arts or popular music, for example. But all the ways you amend your internal systems or make networking contacts or change your financial reporting internally are all creative tasks. If you find yourself tinkering with aspects of the business most people would think are settled and done, long after your team has gone home, this is a good sign you are entrepreneurially creative. It is the unique application of those many hundreds of combined improvements that makes a business successful.

If you find yourself asking yourself 'What if we . . . ?' rather than simply accepting the way things are done, maybe you are an entrepreneur after all.

1.4 Improving Processes as You Go Along

It's not all about inventing things and technological know-how. In fact, good entrepreneurship is mostly about processes – the way things get done, commercially.

It always used to puzzle me that if the theory about providing the best-quality product for the appropriate problem was the answer to being successful, then why aren't all businesses making consistent profits and staying in business forever? Quality is easy to copy and measure in most industries. You can buy guides about quality to get it commercially right.

But the truth is that quality really means the sum total of all the things you do and how they combine to give a result. That includes the human bit and relationships. It's not just about the physical product or your new machine or your prices.

At a guess, there are probably a couple of hundred processes a small business undertakes in the profit cycle, which include finding a client right through to the invoice and after-sales support. These activities can easily include establishing a brand or a presence in the marketplace, techniques to approach new clients or responding to repeat clients, making the product or delivering the service, costing the contract, completing the job, invoicing the job, and collecting the money you are owed.

In addition, there are all the processes the client probably never sees, such as hiring and firing employees, complying with current legislation, managing internal finance, fostering good relations internally and externally, managing the premises, and dealing with legal issues.

In any given period, I would guess that 60% of your time is taken up with these 'hidden processes', leaving just 40% for actually doing the work. The trick is to do these hidden processes as efficiently as possible, so they do not become a drag on producing quality products or services. Or talking to new clients.

But be careful! It can be very tempting to bury oneself in administrative tasks and fool yourself into thinking you are very busy. In fact, you are probably wasting a lot of time trying to be perfect in ways that no one will ever see. You may be failing at the things that will really make a difference to the business. Like networking.

1.5 Are You a Risk-Taker?

Another common misunderstanding about running a successful business is whether you are willing to take risks. Over the years, people have said to me, 'Oh, I could never do what you do. . . . I would worry about losing money or being out of a job'.

In my mind, risk can always be calculated immediately as being worth it or not, in any given situation. An entrepreneurial mindset will investigate the positives and negatives, weigh up the downsides carefully, and then decide how much to invest in the new idea or way of doing things. Often, the best decision is to do nothing for now . . . until you get better information.

The more research you do, the more likely you will come to the logical conclusion that it is often better to risk than not take any risks at all.

In fact, it is often financially more secure to invest in a better outcome than stick with what you are doing and hope for the best. If you stand still, the chances are, you are actually going backwards, bearing in mind the speed of your competition in the market. Any good idea can be quickly copied by your competitors – and often is!

It's all about control. Gone are the days when anyone had a job for life. Even if you work for the government or an established institution, there is an increasing likelihood that central policy will change and you will suddenly find yourself unemployed. Surely, it is better to control the factors that create security for you and your family, rather than just hope someone else makes the right decision for you!

In terms of downsides, it is easy to calculate the cost of 'doing something' and the money being potentially wasted. But if you don't invest, you will lose out in the long run.

Good example: You don't have enough new customers to replace the ones who don't buy again. You can either improve your paid-for marketing or employ another sales representative. Both options will cost money up front, and you will not know for several months what the better option was. But you can be certain that if you do nothing, things won't change and you will be worse off in a few months' time.

Risk is an attitude of mind. You need to be confident that taking action is, in fact, in your interest in the long term. It's a mindset that it needs nurturing. It needs to be part of your plan for the future. If taking risks fills you with dread and possibly makes you ill, then running a small business is not a life choice I would recommend. You will be calculating risk every day as a small business owner. Some big, some small.

Most business decisions I made were 50/50. There was rarely a right or wrong answer that was obvious. You just have to make the call. Then move on.

1.6 Calm in the Face of Adversity

In business as well as in life, panic is rarely the best option. When something goes wrong, do you immediately rush about blindly, trying to fix it, or, worse, still blame other people or your suppliers for the mistake? In any given week, many things will 'go wrong'. But it's how you deal with the situation that defines your suitability to be an entrepreneur.

It is in the nature of providing a service or a product that you will be working with a chain of people who need to deliver their bit so that you can do yours. Depending on how many organisations there are in the chain, mistakes will be common. What matters is that your way of doing things has already factored this into the delivery, through quality control measures or simply having a plan in place to put things right when they go wrong.

Most errors can be predicted. An entrepreneur will already have anticipated how to fix them, even before they happen. When things do go wrong, the important thing for the client is to know that the reaction of the business is calmness and control. That way, the client knows things will be put right. They get what they paid for, even if it wasn't the first time around.

If you are suited to entrepreneurship, you will be able to file those mistakes away as being dealt with or as a useful learning experience so you can do it better next time. Errors are often an opportunity to improve your processes. Nobody deliberately makes mistakes – why would you? So improving the system is the way to go.

Agonising about what went wrong or conducting a 'blame game' is unproductive. If mistakes worry you so much that you begin to micro-manage all the processes of your business, being an entrepreneur may not be for you. You will simply run out of time and probably willing employees to work with you. Good management is getting things done through other people, even if they and you sometimes get it wrong. If you end up doing everything yourself, you may as well work from home and be a sole trader.

1.7 Customer Service Mentality

Business people often get bad press for taking advantage of customers' ignorance or hiking up their profits when an opportunity arises. Quite rightly so. You are very unlikely to get any recommendations or a second sale from that customer if that is your default attitude to customers or clients. But this is not normal for a successful entrepreneur.

Whether you are selling a physical product or your expertise, satisfying the buyer is what should drive you forward. There is an enormous amount of pleasure to be had from offering something to a customer, delivering it as promised, and being paid in full for your efforts. It all amounts to using your skills and doing something meaningful with your life.

Admittedly, some of the benefit accrues to you and your family through remuneration and profits, eventually. But doing a good job and hopefully being asked to do it again is the key to finding the inner reserves to continue to run a business. Every day you have to climb that hill again. If you don't enjoy this challenge, you probably won't enjoy being an entrepreneur. No professional footballer, however talented, expects to win every game.

1.8 Obsessed with 'To-Do' Lists

It is often remarked that if you do not know where you are going, how will you know when you have arrived?

The same is true for business owners who want to stay in business beyond the end of the month. You need a plan, if only to measure how you are doing. People often resist making a plan because, they say, so many things could change that the plan itself is just a pipe dream. That may be so if the plan does not deliver what you want. But you will never know how to improve things if you have no plan to begin with. You respond to the last bad thing that happened, often out of all proportion to the perceived issue.

Entrepreneurs are natural list-makers and preparers, always thinking what comes next, the what-ifs and the how-tos. Even if such thoughts are not written down in a spreadsheet, the ideas are plans in themselves. Ideally, you would formalise the ideas by costing them out, putting a timescale behind them, and managing things to happen in the right sequence. This is called a budget. It shows where you are going and how you intend to get there.

1.9 Attitude to Money and Investment

However good your ideas are or your empathy with potential customers, you will not get very far without cash flow. In general, customers tend to pay only when the job is finished, and often several months after you have asked them for the money. Some of them go bust and may never pay you at all. That's business.

In an absolute start-up situation, you will need to fund yourself, your team, and your essential suppliers for at least the first quarter of your new venture's life – and, in practice, much longer if your customer typically is a large enterprise. However pleased they may be with your product or service, the wheels of large corporates grind slowly. A first-time supplier is unlikely to be paid immediately, on demand. So you need a cash float to keep you going.

Where does this money come from? It could be from your savings, in which case it only costs you lost savings account interest. It could come from a loan from family, which again may be cost-neutral to the business.

It could come from an investment from someone outside the family. Assuming you have given them a small proportion of your shares or some other financial deal, there will be no need to pay it back until perhaps your new venture is sold.

But beware: this would be typical of a VC (venture capitalist). The downside is that they will take a keen commercial interest in how you are doing almost daily and want to be involved in any major business decisions, which could be very irritating for you as you try to get the thing off the ground.

There will always be plenty of people willing to criticise what you are doing. It takes time to explain to them why you did what you did. Often, the critics are only aware of one aspect of the situation. If they knew the whole story, they would see it was a judgement call. They would probably have done what you did in the same circumstances.

1.10 Bank Loans

The more likely scenario for raising cash is a bank loan at commercial rates, backed by some kind of asset, typically your home or other asset. This arrangement will probably be agreed for at least a year. The bank will have studied your business plan, especially the generation of income, and be eager to talk about any negative deviations from the plan.

Banks get bad press when it comes to supporting businesses, as they tend not to lend to anyone unless they already have assets they can retrieve from you should things go wrong. But what banks have is lots of experience of lending to many thousands of small businesses. This means they are in a good position to see if your plans will work out, statistically speaking. If they won't lend you any money, it is very likely your plan is not quite right yet. It's nothing personal. They are a business as well. They cannot afford to have too many bad loans in their business plan.

In all these borrowing scenarios, you will have to deal with the pressure of 'interested parties' wanting to know if their money is safe. As you will discover later, there are hundreds of issues to deal with when setting up a business, not the least of which is acquiring customers. These tasks need to be prioritised over giving a running commentary to partners and institutions about how things are going every few days.

Not everyone finds managing finance easy to deal with. If you have spent all your life until now living within your means, avoiding credit, and paying bills early, the entrepreneurial life may not suit you.

As you might expect, the bigger the business, the more likely that financial pressures will be bigger, as investors have more to lose. You will need to somehow compartmentalise the large financial numbers you will be dealing with in trading from your everyday financial life. It's okay to approve several hundred thousand for new plant and yet still worry about the cost of the weekly shopping trolley. If you can do this without anxiety and you can separate the two, this is a measure of your psychological resilience.

1.11 Psychological Resilience

Running a small business – in fact, running any business – will become an obsession. It will consume almost all your waking hours and most of your dreams, whether you remember them or not. Your holidays will be spent sneaking a look at your devices to find out how things are going. You will have already sussed out where you can get access to business services, even in the most remote hotel in the world. You will feel lost if you don't know the week's sales figures.

When you're home, you will want to 'keep in touch' at the weekend and make yourself available if things need discussing, at any time. Unlike the salaried equivalent role, you are never offline if urgent things have to be discussed or decided. You will know that a text or a voice call at the right moment to the right person could save you hundreds or earn you thousands, regardless of the time of the day or night. I often think of professional sports teams when it comes to psychological resilience. The best team in the league sometimes loses a match, often to mediocre opposition. Mentally, you need to be able to examine why you lost, dust yourself down, and 'go again'. No one becomes ineffective overnight. Mistakes can happen. It does not mean your team or your business has suddenly become a failure.

In the final analysis, as an entrepreneur, it's your plan, your money, and possibly your family's future well-being at stake when you are running a small business. If you're happy to take on that challenge and run those calculated risks and enjoy doing it, day in, day out . . . congratulations!

It may just be that you really are made of the right stuff.

But nothing happens in business without people. It may seem obvious, but without the right people in place, no business can prosper. If you can only trust yourself to get things done to your level of quality, you are a sole trader, not an entrepreneur of a small business.

In the next chapter, I deal with what to look for when recruiting your team and how to manage the inevitable shortfalls in small business performance.

KEY LEARNINGS

- Average at words and numbers but better at selling/presenting/explaining.
- Interested in improving the way things get done, commercially.
- Happy to take reasonable risks, as long as they are in your favour.
- Calm in the face of adversity.
- Enjoy the challenge of delighting customers, depending on budget.

- Habitual list-maker and planner; little left to chance.
- Positive attitude to debt, investment, and stakeholders.
- Psychologically strong; can handle stress positively.
- Happy to say, after a mistake, 'We go again!'

Note

1 Hillel the Elder.

Chapter 2

Businesses Are about People

Here's one of my pet phrases: *businesses do not make profits; people do.* There are very few small businesses where you do not need to rely on other human beings to create and deliver things or services for your customers. The success of your business relies on other people outside your enterprise doing what they do best, whatever that is. But how do you get the best out of them, and what do you do if they are not delivering?

Most new businesses grow organically in the early years. Your first employee may be your life partner or a good friend. Subsequent team members may be friends of friends who heard about your venture informally. It may be a good few years before you need to think about how to recruit the right team and start to use professional recruitment agencies.

But long before then, your overriding aim should be to think about the succession plan. In other words, when you come to sell the business, will there be individuals in place to do what you do or what your most trusted team member does? This will be the last thing on your mind when you start

DOI: 10.4324/9781003532118-3

out. But it becomes ever more important as you try to grow the business and eventually approach the time to sell it.

2.1 Defining the Role for New Team Members

It's easy to say, but every business needs an onboarding plan. Few have one.

There will come a time when you've simply got to have more people. The days of relying on family and friends have gone. It may be that you need specific skills, such as accounting. Or you need another pair of hands to get around all the prospects your reputation is producing. Sometimes it may be a replacement you need when someone leaves unexpectedly.

People with a corporate human resources background will ask you for the role profile. This is the way to do it. You need to describe the role rather than the person who used to do it. It may be tempting to simply hire a clone of the last person if you were happy with what they did. But it often surprised me that a new person often brought other skills I had not considered before which could be part of the new role.

The profile of the role should include things like core admin skills, especially being computer literate, a positive personality, ability to work flexibly – projects do not always come in with plenty of time to get them done. You should define the key parts of the job for it to be a success in your eyes. In addition, they should meet the basic 'hygiene' requirements, such as living relatively locally, being able to drive, having a generally good health and a collaborative personality.

In the final analysis, the best candidate is not always the one with the most impressive academic background or on paper experience. One reason they are in the job market again may be that they are just not very good at it. Personal skills go a long way to helping your business be more successful. What you need are *people* people, first and foremost.

2.2 Using a Recruitment Agency

It is tempting to think that after several years running your own business, you have enough local contacts and a wide-enough network of acquaintances to be able to find the right candidate. But there is never enough time in the working day to make the right calls, remain discrete, follow up friendly suggestions, have the initial discussion, then organise for the candidate to have a remote video call or even visit your premises. You may find yourself spending more time recruiting than dealing with new clients, which is never a good thing for a business with limited resources.

So using an agency is the answer. But just be careful about the fees. It is not unusual to find yourself paying 20% − 25% or more of the advertised salary when you appoint your next team member. Better still, put this allowance into your annual budget plan on the basis that you will need to recruit X number of people during the year, if you are going to achieve your targets. If you don't spend it, then that's cash saved, so more profit for the business.

The advantage of agencies is that they normally have a database of likely candidates already on file. They can obviously work on any candidates you can give them too. The point is that they take all the admin out of contacting people and assessing whether they are the right fit for your business. The better your written profile, the more likely they will find you suitable candidates that make sense for your enterprise.

The second key point about agencies is that they are normally remunerated on a successful appointment. They have a vested interest in getting someone in position quickly, so they are motivated to get things moving rather than delay things, as happens if you try to do it yourself. There will always be something more urgent for you to do than having an exploratory chat with a prospective, new team member.

The third factor is that agencies normally provide more than one candidate, as they know that however good a candidate may be on paper, they may just not fit as a personality in real life. There may not be something you can put your finger on immediately. It could simply be a feeling that the person is not quite right for you at that particular moment. Or more likely, a good candidate will have more than one offer and they may choose someone else after stringing you along for several weeks for reasons known only to themselves.

2.3 Interviewing for a Small Business Position

Assuming the agency has been briefed properly and the candidates have done their homework on you and your business, the interview, preferably in person, is crucial in whether the person will fit into your existing team. After all, you are running a joint venture, so to speak, where several people must work with each other to get the best overall result.

Things to look out for are being on time for the meeting, giving a positive first impression, having engaging social skills, and most important of all, listening. So many candidates feel they need to be in presentation mode and so forget to stay quiet when you want to talk. It may be that there are some specific tasks or experience that you want to emphasise, unknown to the recruitment agent, which would be a deal-breaker for you.

Perhaps the role involves attendance at a remote meeting place every month, so having a car is essential? Maybe technical familiarity with a certain item of software would be highly desirable to do the job efficiently? Possibly, experience of managing people remotely would be key to success in the role? Whatever the skill is, it needs to come across in the interview as non-negotiable if the discussions are to progress.

However impressive the candidate may be, it is important not to offer the job to the first person who vaguely fits the job description. Chances are that if they are impressive at first glance, they will also have been impressive at their other interviews. They may already have accepted another role elsewhere, so they are, in fact, interviewing you! The best strategy is to conduct all the interviews and promise candidates a date by which you will draw up a shortlist, even if you only have two likely candidates.

2.4 Does Your Candidate Imagine Themself Doing the Job?

There is always the inevitable part of any interview where you give the candidate the chance to ask questions of you. All candidates realise this is part of the process, and they normally prepare a few questions in advance. If they have no questions, I think you can deduce they have already had an offer elsewhere, as it suggests they don't imagine themselves ever actually doing the job for you. Anyone who asks practical questions about the role probably indicates the candidate is actively considering the role, such as details of expenses, holiday dates they may have pre-booked, or travelling considerations. If they are imagining themselves doing the role, it's a very good sign that they want the job.

The more of a conversation the interview is, the more likely the candidate will be a good fit. If you find it hard going and find yourself hoping the interview will come to an end sooner rather than later, then perhaps the candidate has the wrong personality for your business.

One further word of caution: It may be that you come across an interviewee who is fresh out of college, has top grades in their business qualifications, and is overwhelmingly enthusiastic about how they perceive your industry and your specific business. It is possible they will turn out to be the best team member you have ever had. But it is more likely that they will become bored after a few months and realise they were looking for another kind of opportunity, perhaps in a large multinational, with more career prospects.

The interview process is as much about how the candidate will match what you are offering at their point in their career as what role you need to fill. Be honest and help them make the right decision for themselves and for you.

Finally, make sure you have a plan to tell candidates your decision in a timely and professional manner. There is nothing worse than simply securing the best candidate for you and ignoring all the others. It does your reputation as a local employer great harm to leave unsuccessful candidates in no-man's-land, where they have to chase you for a decision.

At the very least, provide helpful notes for your agency or the candidates themselves as to why they were not successful, whether that be for a technical reason or simply that there was a better candidate that time. Chances are that you will be hiring again within the same professional pool a year or so later. People will remember how they were treated the first time around. We all know that bad impressions are eagerly shared amongst many peers, which will make your ability to recruit similar people more difficult the second time around.

2.5 Onboarding Is Not Just for Big Organisations

Onboarding is the relatively recent way of describing how an organisation goes about blending new recruits into an organisation or business that has hired them. For the new recruit, it is a time of maximum optimism and some trepidation as to whether they have made the right decision to quit their old job and start afresh somewhere new.

To make sure that new recruits retain their enthusiasm, you need an onboarding plan that introduces them to the wider business while providing them with learning opportunities to get up to speed in their specific role. This series of activities is not going to happen by chance, although too many employers do not plan the assimilation of new team members beyond 30 minutes of general introduction and coffee with their line manager, if they have one. Most new recruits have more meaningful contact with your IT consultant than anyone else in the entire organisation.

The first things to prepare for are the basics.

Where are they going to sit?. Will they need a new desk? Can they get access to the IT system? Can software training, if needed, be provided from day 1? Will they need a laptop for remote working? Or a cell phone? Do we have all their personal details to remunerate them? Do they have an employment contract? Have they seen the team handbook? Is there a list and job functions of team colleagues to hand? What expectations should they have for their working hours/breaks, and does this change on certain days, such as weekends or national holidays?

Every business has its own ways of working, so it is important not to assume that the new recruit knows them all or knows as many as are relevant to being able to do a good job.

Part of any good onboarding plan is to cover all the support they will need to be effective within a programme of learning from the very first day. Typically, this will involve an overview of the business or even the industry sector from senior people who are respected within the organisation for their knowledge. It could be you, the owner. Or it may be someone designated as the human resources executive. Or it may be your best operator.

There should then be some formal IT training, if only to be able to log on securely to access various files which will no doubt be needed for the tasks to be done.

The main point is that new people should feel welcomed and prepared for rather than their arrival being a big surprise and creating panic measures, which is what happens in many small businesses – and some large ones!

2.6 Think about How New Recruits Will Fit In

It's inevitable that your ideal job profile will not be met, simply because you don't have access to every possible perfect candidate at any one time. In fact, the perfect candidate may not actually exist. You will be interviewing candidates who are available and probably local in most circumstances. That means you may have to make a trade-off between someone who fits all the technical criteria and another candidate who has other skills you need for the role.

We once interviewed for a financial manager. We had two equally qualified and experienced possibles. The only difference was personality. One was very easy to get on with and somewhat compliant to any view which was discussed. They had a service mentality. The other was more aggressive and tended to offer an alternative view of any financial situation. We were gearing ourselves up for a potential purchase of another business at that time which would be headed up by the finance team, and this person would lead the process.

On balance, we thought the more 'difficult' candidate would suit us better in negotiations and efficiency. It turned out to be true. They had a cutting edge which served us well over the next ten years which the other candidate would not have had. If we had hired the easy-going candidate, it would have been up to the owners to ask all the difficult financial questions. That's great, but it can be tiring if you are always the one who has to be doubtful about any new business proposition or process. Being negative is rarely popular. Raising a possible objection does not mean you don't agree. You just want to have a debate about it. Sometimes, you need to be persuaded to feel better about any major decision, by exploring all the negative options.

2.7 Job Role Descriptions

It is an open secret that most job descriptions are written for recruiting new staff, then largely ignored once they join. This is not surprising, as the new person who joins probably does not possess the perfect competences that the job role is asking for.

What really needs to happen is for the job description to be rewritten, say, three months after the successful new person has joined, if only to measure their performance against things they can achieve. This is a lot of work for a people specialist and requires some discipline to constantly assess what team members are currently doing and assess them accordingly. If you run an annual appraisal system, you will need to do this anyway because team members can only be assessed on what they are doing daily rather than what you think they should be doing in some idealised, perfect world which you have imagined.

On the other hand, it may be that with a number of new recruits all taken on at the same time, you see an unwelcome drift into doing things you never set out to do. Revising job descriptions on a regular basis means you are actively thinking about what you are trying to achieve and remembering to ask team members to adjust to the overall plan, rather than the plan being adjusted to who you happened to employ during the recent period.

Here's an example. An app provider has a marketing plan that says they will target the pharmaceutical market for new process apps, as this sector has high margins and global reach in most medical developments. They struggled to recruit software developers with relevant medical sector experience and have taken on several other sector software team members who just happen to have market-leading automotive sector experience.

Within two years, the business is now totally focussed on automotive clients, to the extent that the relationship networkers (salespeople) have had to learn a completely new way of marketing apps (manufacturer contracts, not pharmaceutical contracts). The result is that the app provider now has very few pharma clients, business margins have plummeted, and at the next funding round, the investors want to know why the strategy going forward has changed.

If job descriptions had been regularly reviewed, the senior team would have seen the drift and been able to assess whether the new direction was one worth pursuing or not. As in all businesses, output all depends on people skills. But you need to monitor those skills against your business plan.

By knowing what your team is actually doing, day by day, not just what their old job descriptions say they are doing, you will be forewarned that the plan is going in a different direction. You may be happy with that. But not if your margins have changed out of all recognition and your investors become unhappy with what you have been doing with their money.

2.8 Monitoring Performance

In a perfect world, new team members slot in perfectly, know how to do everything immediately, and become efficient and effective within days. But life is not really like that. Over the years of taking on many new people, I have noticed a sharp difference between how the interviewee performed at the interview and how they performed in the first few weeks. This period of onboarding needs careful monitoring so as not to lose that initial enthusiasm everyone has when starting a new job.

It is quite likely that a new recruit may have exaggerated their IT skills at the interview. Training them in your particular systems is an important element in making them feel welcome. Don't assume they know what to do. One person's detailed report is another person's short overview. You need to be very clear about what is expected for each element of the job and show them examples of what output you are looking for. They cannot guess if you don't tell them.

You will have existing templates for many of the processes in your organisation. Make sure the new recruit not only has full access to the software but also keeps to the template. Hopefully, they will have some ideas as to how to improve them. But get the new team member to discuss and share. Otherwise, you will end up with different types of documentation going around the business. People will become frustrated if the 'new documentation' misses out some older, vital steps which other departments used to rely on to get the job done efficiently.

No one wants to be negative. But it would be a truly gifted new employee who gets everything right from day 1. Set up a weekly review in their first month so they can ask questions or voice opinions. You may not agree with all of them, but at least you know what their perspective is. I would even suggest that these weekly reviews continue until you both decide they are no longer necessary.

Line managers should certainly be reviewing the performance of all team members every three months in private so they can voice any concerns or simply to get feedback on how they are doing. It is surprising how many employees do not realise they are under-performing in the eyes of the business until they are told. This does not need to be over-critical and can be done in a constructive way. You both want their performance to be the best that it can possibly be, after all. No one is going to be let go for making one mistake. But the only way they will know they are making mistakes is if someone tells them.

2.9 Disciplining Under-Performance

It is a shame that human resource departments and professionals the world over tend to use aggressive, legal language when team members consistently under-perform. *Discipline. Warning. Formal interview. Dismissal. . . . 'Would you like another member of staff to witness this procedure?'*

It is a fact that sometimes individuals have oversold themselves at interview. After a few months, they realise they do not have the right skills or perhaps the enthusiasm to continue in the role they were offered. Before you decide to give them notice, explore whether there is another role they might be very good at.

Someone with competent technical knowledge may have been taken on as a salesperson because they were good at explaining at interview how a particular product worked. But they turned out to be hopeless at networking or going through the necessary processes to find new clients. It does not make them a bad person.

Perhaps there is a role for a technically competent person with people skills in your business, where they could be effectively employed? You have probably paid a substantial sum to the recruitment firm to acquire this team member, so it would be expensive just to discard them without exploring all the internal options.

If they are just simply not good enough for the particular role or, indeed, any other role, it's time to say goodbye and put it down to experience.

2.10 Provide Opportunities to Improve

Legislation is tight these days about letting people go. The potential costs of litigation if you get it wrong is a strong reason for most employers to take great care should you decide you would like to cut your losses.

Everyone has the right to know they are under-performing, to see if they can improve. So the first step is always to give the team member the opportunity to put things right or change their attitude if this is really what's wrong. A month is a good period to suggest, for two reasons.

First, it takes some time to review job performance if it is part of an ongoing business process; a week is not long enough. Secondly, it gives the employee time to consider if this is a role they really want to keep and, if not, to look for another role elsewhere.

If they resign without any trauma and disruption to the rest of the team, then both parties win. Should there be any litigation at some future date, you will, at the very least, be seen to have taken reasonable steps to assist the recruit to improve things.

2.11 Second Interview

If things have not improved, the second interview needs to be short, to the point, and legally compliant. Have a witness in the discussion, such as your finance manager or their direct line manager, to keep a record of what was said. Things can get very heated if it is one-to-one, and two people often have different recollections of who said what in private, if only to support their own viewpoint.

At the end of the interview, you should give clear instructions as to what happens next, to avoid disruption to the rest of the workforce. This should include payment for any notice period, holidays calculation, what to do about laptops or cell phones, and any commission or bonuses due.

In my experience, team members who are dismissed should leave immediately rather than the end of the day, week, or month and be supervised when clearing their workstation by their line manager. A disgruntled employee can do a lot of damage if left alone for a few hours while still logged into the IT system.

2.12 Providing a Reference

One human thing to mention? A reference. However incompetent you think they may have been – possibly their fault, possibly not – everyone deserves a reference to help them find another position. Unless the performance was in some way bordering on criminality, you should provide an objective reference for them to take away. This could be a simple statement of what their job role was and how long they worked for you. It need not contain any value judgements about their performance or why they left. That is up to any new employer to ask them about or pursue. Again, litigation could be threatened if you make any comments in writing about why they left which are not supported by the facts.

2.13 How Can You Provide a Reasonable Reference If the Person Was Dismissed Due to Incompetence?

The standard question you will be asked as an employer by a new employer is usually, 'Would you hire this person again?' It is perfectly acceptable to reply, 'Yes, of course, but not as a salesperson.' Or 'No problem, but not in the finance department.' Let the new employer then take their own view about whether they want to still employ that person. Don't get into a long exchange of emails about specific individuals who have left the organisation. It provides no benefit to you. It is up to the new employer to assess that person's credentials and decide to hire or not hire.

I remember once I had to dismiss a salesman because sales were consistently below par. A few weeks later, I was contacted by their new employer, who asked for a reference. I simply said that I would happily employ this person again, but not in a sales role. Clearly, this did not go down well with the new employer, who had already taken on the candidate as a salesperson and was rather late in checking the references.

The point is, you should always ask for references before you employ someone new and be prepared for a negative response from their previous employer. After all, they left for a reason. In this case, it was because they were not up to the sales task in our type of organisation. This should not stop them from being a success somewhere else.

2.14 Taking Over Another Business

People issues take on another dimension when you are about to acquire a new business (see Chapter 8). If the business is in another country or on a different site, then it is less likely that you will need to lose team members, as there is bound to be some duplication of roles. But if another business is being absorbed into your own on the same site or premises, as in the case of a merger, say, then you need to plan how you want this to pan out.

Finance and IT roles may be the obvious ones that are duplicated. It may be that you can find them alternative roles within the new, merged organisation. But the higher the level, the less likely this is. This may also apply to senior sales roles. There is no escaping from the fact that it may be too expensive to keep two senior people employed at the same firm. Equally, part of the merger plan may well be to 'save costs'. This means inevitably losing experienced people.

You will need to think through the process of letting these people go and providing adequate compensation and references. Getting this wrong can be very expensive should the discussions become litigious. It may leave a somewhat-nasty taste going forward when what you really want is that the two organisations work together in harmony.

Armed with an onboarding plan and a team that, eventually, gels well together, the next missing item for sustained success is the in-house ability to create new sales. The best mousetrap builder in the world is no good if no one knows about it. Many technically superb businesses fail because they did not tell anyone how good their products were.

KEY LEARNINGS

- People make the difference in any business, so choose carefully.
- Never too early to think about your succession plan for key roles.
- Do a proper onboarding plan, whether you have new hires or not.
- Use a recruitment agency; their contacts and expertise will save you time and money.
- A conversational approach to interviews works better than a list of '20 questions'.
- Do your new recruits fit with the future of the business and the current team?
- Before you let someone go, is there another role they could usefully do?
- If you are buying a business, will you still need all the new senior people?

Chapter 3

A Sustainable Small Business Needs Sales

Whichever way you cut it, sales are what make for a successful business. No amount of technical ability, investment, qualified people, or know-how is of any use to you unless you have a process for making new sales. Because however brilliant your products and services are, clients and customers do not always buy initially or again, for all kinds of reasons.

You need to make the numbers add up or you will soon have no business to manage. In brief, your business plan is *sales less costs equals profit*. Sales are a major part of that plan, but often they are left to chance or, worse still, to the most junior people in the business.

3.1 Why Have a Sales Strategy

Most small businesses begin with acquiring a new client almost by accident, doing what is necessary to provide your product for that client, and then being introduced to another client by the original client. A classic referral cycle.

 DOI: 10.4324/9781003532118-4

The problem comes when you have finished that big job you were so excited about a couple of months ago. But then you find you have no more new projects. There is often a panic to look around for new clients. Your experience tells you that it takes at least a month, if not longer, to find and confirm a new client project. The bigger the client, the more likely this will take several months. Meanwhile, you have bills to pay and a team to keep busy and motivated.

It would be much better to have a regular supply of new clients, regardless of any current work projects, so that when one job finishes, another job can begin. This is called a sales strategy.

3.2 Key Elements in the Sales Plan

Everyone will tell you that selling your services or product into any market is unique and tailored to each need. They may say that having a sales process is very difficult to define or even maintain. So why not just hope for the best and 'work hard'? Working hard does not guarantee success. In fact, simply putting the hours in is more likely to lead to the business going bust more quickly than taking time out to plan for sales.

What elements should you have to create ongoing sales? The first thing to write down is a clear proposition. What is it that you are offering, and have you explained it clearly to people who may want to buy? Done that? Good. But how do prospective buyers know about you?

3.3 Website Presence

These days, a website is the first thing a prospective buyer will consult if they are in the market for what you can provide. Brochures are fine, but they soon go out of date and often they fail to define exactly what you do, after a few months. It is true to say that at the outset of any business, you do not really know what your best service or product is, even if it is something everyone apparently understands, such as plumbing or working in retail.

If you are providing services directly into the home, registering with a national accredited site can promote your services in a quick and simple way. But buyers will still be on the lookout for your own website so they can see what it is you do best. In a world of influencers and advice providers, you need to have somewhere to control what is accurate about your business.

Taking the lead from marketers, you could do worse than define your product in terms of the main things you provide, the price of those products, and examples of satisfied customers. This is the bare minimum that buyers will want to know. Your contact details are essential, cell number, address, pictures of premises, if relevant. But also, tell them how you will contact them if they leave their details. Too many sites are full of pretty pictures but fail to say what happens next, from the customer's viewpoint.

3.4 Lead Generation System

Part of your website must be a way to capture prospect or buyer information in a way that is easy to complete and, above all, non-threatening. Visitors to the site can be tracked with hidden software, so knowing that someone has been looking is useful, even if you do not initially follow them up. With a list of their details, you are also able to analyse the sort of person who is looking and so tweak your offer accordingly. Websites are easy to amend, unlike printed materials, so editing your offer and responding to the main reasons people are looking make perfect marketing sense.

But be careful. You need to gather as much information as possible before changing things. For example, there may be some kind of government publicity about what you do, and so you will get all kinds of searches – journalists, public service employees, students, concerned parents, and some visitors simply looking for free advice. They may not be buyers at all. You can waste a lot of time being the main point of contact for a trade or industry journal but never actually communicating with any potential customers.

The categories to take notice of are enquirers who become clients, the industry sector they work in, and possibly the size of their own client enterprise. This knowledge helps you decide how to pitch your offer in the future. Contrary to what you first thought, it may be that most enquirers and buyers turn out to be, say, medium-sized local businesses looking for a local supplier. Or perhaps they are mostly one-off consumer clients with a need for a quick solution? Whatever it turns out to be, the examples may be so dominant that you then decide to change your promotion on the website to attract even more of that type of client.

Alternatively, you may decide that you want a specific type of client who you know would pay well for your skills – in other words, a higher margin of profit. The solution is to reword your website to appeal to only those who fit your new criteria, which by default would put off less-lucrative prospects. No point in chasing for business you do not really want or cannot support professionally. Do not be a slave to your website – if it is delivering the wrong kind of enquiries, just change it!

3.5 Outsourced Lead Providers

It is highly likely that however good your website is, it will never generate enough enquiries by itself to keep your enterprise afloat. The more successful you are, the more operational people you will need, and so the more enquiries you will need to keep them busy and profitable. The cycle goes on, and the machine needs to be fed. The main function of the website is to be your shop window, so prospects can see what you do, rather than a deliverer of all your leads. In my experience, only about 10% of business is generated by a good website, but not much more. You need other mechanisms to create new sales.

Before you decide to employ your own sales or representation team, you may be tempted to outsource the prospecting process to an external supplier. It will certainly be less expensive than employing people yourself. You can save costs quickly by simply stopping or halting the service if it is not working.

Is outsourcing the sales process the answer? Probably not, in the long term. Initially, there is a lot of 'training' to be done, as the outsourced agency does not know the ins and outs of your business. This means several briefing sessions by you for their team before they can even hit the email lists or phones. They are usually very good at reporting on how many people they have contacted and what was said. Not so good at closing the sale.

Profitable results are usually hard to come by. It is likely they will be able to get appointments for you, if you sell a professional service. But then you need to factor in that only one in five prospects will actually buy something, if you are lucky. That means they will probably need to research many hundreds of names, speak to only 10% of them, and make appointments with less than 3%. It is time-consuming work and needs to be done relentlessly if it is going to be profitable for you. Do not expect any results for at least three months, probably longer.

If they are good on the phone, then they will certainly get agreement to meetings. But there is usually a high level of cancellations the day before, when prospects realise what they have said yes to. Inevitably, there will be no-shows – the prospect is simply not there anymore or unavailable when you come to call.

The only way to make this service pay for you is to agree to a deal based on actual sales, not just appointments. For most lead agencies, this model will not work for them because they will argue that how well you convert the appointments is not in their control. They are unprepared to be remunerated only on that basis. But it is worth asking for a hybrid solution.

Taking into account a full year's activity and being consistent about reviewing the lead supplier's performance, you can probably count on 10% of your sales leads coming from this activity. That is good in the sense that all you need to do is turn up for the online or in-person appointment to present your services. But what about the other sales you need?

The only sure-fire way to generate a predictable level of sales is to have your own sales team.

3.6 Your Own Sales Team

You have probably been the only and best salesperson in your enterprise, up until now. Maybe you share this task with another founder or senior employee because you know your products best. But you are never going to grow the business fast enough that way for it to be worth very much – there are far too many other issues that need dealing with once the first few clients are on board or after you have achieved a certain level of repeating sales turnover.

Growing sales is best done with sales specialists whose job is clearly defined as getting more clients . . . and nothing else. In many businesses, extremely good project managers are expected to get new clients as part of their job description. But this rarely happens, even with a willing team. When there is a choice between making a prospective sales call and doing something operational, most team members will opt for the operational task. There is always work to be done with what you have already without adding the specialised job of cold or warm selling.

3.7 What Makes for a Good Salesperson?

People with great sales skills are a riddle, wrapped in a mystery, inside an enigma, to paraphrase Sir Winston Churchill. Apart from a good track record, it is notoriously difficult to spot a good salesperson before they start doing it. No amount of psychological testing or interviewing will ever predict who will be successful for you in your particular type of work.
In most cases, you will not know for more than six months whether they are or can be successful in that role. It is a question of gut feel and faith in the process of selling. Plus good training, of course.

3.8 What Makes for an Effective Salesperson?

For a start, at interview, are they empathetic? By that I mean are they easy to talk to? Do they listen to you when you are talking? Do they ask insightful questions, which show they are thinking about working for you? If they do, this is a good start.

Are they well-organised? Did they turn up on time, were they well-presented, had they good examples to show about their accomplishments? These are all factors which show an organised mindset for a specific task rather than just playing things by ear and hoping for the best.

Do they do sports? This is not an absolute necessity, but over the years I have noticed that good salespeople are often actively involved in sport. Maybe it makes sense because most sport is competitive and involves repeating tasks until you get some success – just like sales. But sport also usually involves meeting up and playing with other people on a regular basis. This suggests they actually like meeting and interacting with others and would do it, whether they got paid for it or not. It is a mistake to think everyone enjoys putting themselves in new social situations, which is what most salespeople need to do every day.

Are they okay with numbers? There are many aspects of business where being quick with numbers can be an advantage. It is surprising how many normal people do not understand percentages, for example, and would happily offer a buyer a 100% discount (this means no cost) to get the business!

The final test is whether they are persistent or not. Is there any evidence in their résumé that they keep going at something when perhaps the average person would have given up long ago?

It goes without saying that some sales experience is always useful, together with time spent in your particular business sector. But being an expert in, say, paper bags does not necessarily mean you can sell them. Personal skills are more important than technical knowledge. Most of what a seller needs to know can be taught quite quickly. Do not reject candidates just because they have no direct experience of your market.

3.9 Do You Need More Than One Salesperson?

In my mind, there are two aspects to being an effective salesperson. The first is the drive to approach each day as if anything is possible, because in business it really is. You never know what a prospect will want or even need. Even if you have had no success for the past few months, you need to have a mindset that says perhaps today is the day things might

be different. In terms of activity, a typical seller may have
to contact 100 people to get ten conversations, to get three
costed proposals, resulting in one sale. When you add up all
the effort, many people become overwhelmed by the numbers
and become less and less effective.

The second aspect to being an effective salesperson is good
research. That means the enthusiasm to compile a relevant
database, keep it updated, plan when you are going to establish contact and keep your promises to stay in touch or send
on some relevant product information . . . or simply remaining
in contact. This is not easy, as administration is not usually
what characterises a great salesperson.

That is why employing a pair of sellers with complementary skills often pays dividends. The ideal team would be an
irrepressible contact person who is persistent, together with
a researcher/list manager who understands the overall task.
They may not be someone you would normally send off to a
client meeting to pitch your wares. But you would always rely
on their administration and the ability to spot anomalies or
data mistakes to assist the sales effort.

In addition, selling can be a lonely occupation, as often
they do not have the skills to do the operational tasks that are
being sold. They will have to feel good about handing over
their 'relationship' to other team members who can do the
job well. A team of two people at least who have the overriding task of looking for new clients is the better solution,
even though the costs are more than just taking on one seller.
Hunting together is always more fun than hunting alone.

3.10 Creating the Sales Plan or Strategy

Sales do not happen in isolation. You need to be sure that
your new sales team is talking to the right kind of clients

about the sort of services and products you can actually deliver, at a profit. The market is full of small businesses making unprofitable sales.

In Chapter 5, we will discuss the importance of having an overall business plan. Sales activity is simply one aspect of that strategic plan. But what is a *sales plan*, and how do you focus the sales effort around it?

3.11 Initial Briefings

More than any other department or part of the business, sales activity needs to be completely aligned with the financial aims of the organisation. You can waste a lot of time and resources opening doors to clients for whom you have no suitable solutions at a price they would be willing to pay.

Salespeople need to buy in completely to what the shareholders are trying to achieve. The briefing should follow this kind of pattern.

1. *What does Company X provide in terms of customer or client solutions?*
2. *Whom does it want to sell these products to?*
3. *Which products have the best margins?*
4. *What time of year is best to sell these products?*
5. *If customers buy more than once, what is the process for repeat purchases?*
6. *What promotional support is required to be successful?*
7. *How do we measure success in terms of individual sales and repeat sales?*
8. *Can we use 'happy customer' testimonials?*
9. *What new business sectors could we try?*
10. *Are there any alliances we can develop for other organisations to sell on our behalf?*

This is not an exhaustive list by any means. But it is a starting point. It is always useful to have the key points available to sellers online or in notebook format, so they can remind themselves what the overall purpose of their activity is at any time before they start making contact with potential buyers.

3.12 The Sales Strategy

Now that they have the basic knowledge, they need to be steered in the right direction which will align with the business plan.

Typically, this may be a series of statements with numbers attached where relevant so they fully understand the task required.

For example:

We provide furniture for modern offices to support well-being and health-related objectives.

Our main markets are finance, banking, and data administration organisations who typically employ hundreds of team members at one or several sites.

Our highest-margin products are ergonomic workstations. See attached table of other product margins.

We want to maintain and improve our client retention of 70%, annually.

More than half our revenue is signed up between January and April, annually.

We invest over x thousands each year in B2B promotion and exhibit regularly.

Our reputation as a top 5 supplier helps make us a credible supplier to new and existing clients at premium margins.

Recently, we have been selling significant volumes to educational facilities on request.

The directors are always interested in seeking out new sectors/ relationships at national level.

3.13 Regular Sales Reviews

What needs to happen next is an assessment of what contact activity is needed to support these wishes or outcomes in the form of a promotional plan, a clean database of possible contacts, and regular reviews of contacts, meetings, and actual sales. These reviews are usually a monthly or quarterly sales meeting, together with a financial update on successes and the not-so-successful.

It is clear from this kind of plan that measuring activity is the only sensible way to monitor sales success on the basis that the more targeted and numerous the activities are, the more likely sales will result. But you will need to wait. Corporate budgets are not often left unspent, so you may have to wait until contract renewal time to ensure you have a shot at the next year's budget allocation. They will not all be at the same time, so having your researcher note when this might be is crucial to effective selling in this type of market.

3.14 What Could Possibly Go Wrong?

It would be great if your sales team were perfect at their job, they met the numbers required each month, and you only ever sold high-margin products to easy-to-deal-with buyers.

Unfortunately, business does not work like that. The more likely scenario is that about half of the objectives you set are met and something changes in the market which means you have to adjust your plan. That is fine. No one said it would be plain sailing. But what are the most common problems which come up which will challenge even the most professional sales plan?

■ New Legislation
  Whatever your product or service is, the government is always likely to interfere in the form of new rules and

regulations which will need to be complied with at some stage in the life of any business. Salespeople need to be kept up to date on any pending and actual changes, as their customers all read the newspapers and they will want to know what your business is doing to either comply or mitigate the effects of any new rules.

■ The Economy
Some economists believe that all Western economies go through a seven-year cycle of growth and correction. That means that your sales and plans will be subject to big changes as and when these things happen. The best you can do is be aware of the ups and downs of business life, that it is perfectly normal, and that you may need to refocus your sales team according to what the market is buying out there. If that means letting some people go, that is the nature of running a small business.

■ Losing Salespeople
That said, it may be that you can reinvent your costs for sales and introduce a commission scheme which is results-orientated rather than a fixed cost. Believe it or not, some sellers prefer to be 'freelance', which leaves them free to do other jobs or even take care of sick relatives, for example, while still working for you on a results-only basis. The value to you is you only pay for actual sales rather than the promise of sales. It works well in some industries, but you have no real control over performance. Can your business survive if your freelancers fail to sell?

3.15 Increase in Costs

Many businesses are subject to volatile prices for incoming supplies to which they add value to create their profits. If your incoming costs increase, you will have to cover the cost by more sales, higher prices, or less administration costs. In my experience, saving on organisational costs is the first remedy when external costs increase. Getting rid of sellers is usually the last resort and the beginning of the slide into failure. Because whatever happens, you will always need to generate new sales.

■ Change of Overall Business Strategy
   Sometimes you need to take a good look at the way you are doing business and possibly re-engineer how it works to maintain or increase profits. It is nobody's fault. The wider market moves on, and you need to move with it or die. Tough as it sounds, this may mean losing team members. But it might also mean taking more on, but of a different type. This is one reason it is good to keep in touch with financial institutions and possibly independent wealthy investors. As sure as eggs is eggs, changing the focus of the business is bound to be more expensive than sitting on your hands and hoping for the best. You will need to find the extra cash from somewhere.

3.16 Mergers and Acquisitions

If you buy a business or someone acquires you, there will inevitably be changes to the way your sales are conducted. This is not always negative. Being bought by another business could increase what your sales team can sell, because they may have more products to offer. It may be just what they need to expand their activities. Blending them into the newly expanded organisation is a key task to ensure the success of both organisations. It is something which should be planned for rather than simply be left to the individuals to work out for themselves.

3.17 All Team Members Are Salespeople

It is easy to blame the sales team if the organisation is under-shooting its numbers. After all, they are the ones whose job it is to bring in the contracts so that operational people have work to do. But your 'offer' to clients includes everyone connected with the business, where they come into contact with potential customers or potential clients.

You should review on a regular basis all the touch points with the outside world, such as reception, telephone answering, customer documentation, accounting, and even delivery, if you have physical items to distribute. There is nothing more common than 'brand dissonance', as a business consultant might say; the experience of a buyer jars when they actually try to buy something from you. How often have you been impressed with national advertising for a particular business only to find that when you try to contact them to buy the product or service, they never answer the phone or their billing is always wrong. No amount of professional selling can put this right.

That is why everyone in the business has a duty to know what you are all about, what you are promising the customer, and where you might be able to improve things. Sometimes this is referred to as 'total brand engagement'. It applies to small local businesses as much as to larger corporations. Delight the new customer; do not disappoint them.

3.18 The Importance of Making Profits

We have touched briefly on the importance of salespeople knowing what margins the business is aiming for so that they can sell the right volume of products to create the right level of profits. Because without profits, there is no business and no future employment for anyone, not just the owners. The next chapter deals with probably the most important issue in any successful business: the money and what the numbers mean.

KEY LEARNINGS

- Sales activity is crucial to business success.
- Get your own sales team, probably two; it is much more efficient.
- Write down your sales strategy to support the business plan, and then rewrite it when it does not work.
- Consider what may affect your sales plan, and review regularly.
- Merging with another business may improve your sales efforts.
- All team members are salespeople, regardless of their team role.

Chapter 4

It's the Money, Stupid!

One of my most-used phrases in business conversation comes from the American writer H. L. Mencken:

> *When somebody says it's not about the money, it's about the money.*[1]

Doing a budget and then seeing if you were right is the life-blood of all businesses. Financial planning may well be the last thing you want to spend time on once you feel the excitement of servicing your first customers. The problem lies in the fact that it is relatively easy to acquire new customers if that's what you really enjoy and spend all your time on.

But what happens when you have promised to deliver something but run out of cash before it can be completed? It is a universal truth that, in general, you get paid when the job is complete, not before you start. Cash flow (and money management) is therefore 'king' for small enterprises.

4.1 Cash Management

The main reason small businesses collapse is to do with managing cash, rather than any incompetence or losing customers.

DOI: 10.4324/9781003532118-5

If you planned to have, say, 250,000 in the bank at this time of the year and you only have 100,000, it forces you to think about why that is and what you can do about it, if anything.

It could be that you did not collect as much revenue as you planned for this quarter. (You may want to have a word with your financial team.) Or you had a big purchase and were not expecting to have to pay for it in this particular period. Tax payments to the revenue often fall into this category and rise accordingly with your sales activity, so you may have been a victim of your own, temporary success. Other substantial financial payments can fall due without you realising they are owed, such as insurance renewals, property maintenance charges, or bank loan repayments.

If you hold deposits for your clients, it may be that a supplier has suddenly changed their rules and now wants cash upfront rather than at some later, planned stage, when the job is finished.

But the more likely explanation is that a few big customers have not paid you on time. Or perhaps they are disputing invoices and you were not aware they were even an issue. If you only have three big customers and they all decide to delay paying you during the same period, there won't be enough cash to pay the monthly wage bill 30 days down the line. Suddenly you need a substantial amount of cash that the business simply does not have.

4.2 The Factoring Solution

The instant reaction to this issue for most owners, after thinking about any potential rich relatives, is to seek factoring. Most business banks will offer this service, whereby they will lend you the money in return for control over your invoices and assets. It is often not too onerous in terms of a specific cost. But it is important to check with your customers that this is acceptable. Many large businesses refuse to be invoiced via factoring and may well not do business with you when they realise it. There is still a perception that any business which asks a bank to collect its money is not doing very well if they need to outsource their invoicing.

Factoring your invoices can sometimes suggest to the customer that you are not confident that you will have sufficient cash to pay all your bills each month. As there are many alternative suppliers, out there in the market, customers may decide to deal with someone who does not need to factor their invoices. This also applies to a prospective buyer who may be put off by the fact that you cannot accurately predict your cash flow and would not want to 'get involved' with assigning control over some aspects of your finances to an external institution.

Like any service, factoring also costs money, which is an additional expense to the business. Do you really need to sub-contract your entire revenue collection function to someone outside the business? Or should you be looking at changing your processes so that you don't need a factoring service? Or get yourself a better finance team?

4.3 Payroll Inflation

One of the biggest numbers in any set of management accounts is payroll. At the beginning of the year, you set a budget for payroll based on the people you have and perhaps new people you think you may need to employ during the year. No one knows whether this will be true or not. But if you have a budget, then you can question, on a regular basis, why the numbers do not reflect reality. Or whether you really need these extra people at all.

Most small businesses fall into two categories when it comes to employment plans. The first is that you are so 'successful' with sales that you take on more employees than you need. But by the end of the year, perhaps when the selling season is over, you still have the additional payroll costs which then eat away at your profit.

The second scenario is that you are reluctant to add any more cost to the business, before the new sales uplift has worked its way through the business in terms of customer delivery. This can result in declining quality and possibly low repeat orders because you never seem to have enough resources to deliver what the sales team has created.

Often, as people come and go, you lose track of exactly how many team members you have and the basis on which they were taken on. It's easy to replace a leaver with a more expensive joiner doing the same job. That's fine, if it is just one. But when you acquire three more expensive people for the three inexpensive people that just left, it all begins to add up by the year end. The costs should also include the recruitment fees to acquire them. It only takes five new people at 20% recruitment fee to lose the budget for a complete extra person, over and above the new recruits!

If this is your situation, you may then begin to ask yourself why so many team members are leaving and whether this is 'normal' for your industry or specific to your business. Dealing with churn or employee turnover can be very time-consuming – and expensive.

If you think your recruitment supplier does a good job, then why not discuss a volume deal for the year's hires and try to reduce the fees accordingly? The more they are committed to you in terms of potential fees, the more likely they will supply you with the cream of their candidates.

The other factor that overspending on payroll throws up is your process for hiring. Could it be that your managers are replacing people without proper consultation? As the owner of a small business, you need to take full control of taking on new people. Otherwise, the new contract you have just won on great terms for the business will all be frittered away on indiscriminate hiring costs, just to get the work delivered on time.

It is not unknown for small businesses to take on 'big name' customers in order to get the contract and then struggle to turn a profit on it. Soon you find yourself running a business which is twice the size in terms of sales but no further forward on the bottom line.

This is not always such a bad idea, as generally, the bigger your business volume, the higher the sale price when you come to sell. But a large business making no profit is difficult to sell, unless you are able to admit you are 'mis-managing' it in order to grow it. This is a highly risky strategy, even when the market is good. If you are not making profits, you will have to borrow ever larger sums just to keep paying the bills. A large-volume business making no profits is more of a liability than an asset – it's a collapse waiting to happen.

So if you are in full control of payroll, what else in the budget can go wrong?

4.4 Marketing Spend Creep

Marketing and promotion are usually well-controlled and closely managed in large organizations. They employ specialist technicians to undertake the research and implementation of major marketing spend. The C-suite is often heavily involved in large promotional expenditure, and rightly so. If a campaign goes wrong, it could take years for the brand to recover, not to mention the effect on other brands the organisation owns.

But most small businesses either have no marketing function or have one team member who subcontracts out any major promotion to consultancies and agencies. By looking at the management accounts each month, you can track what the marketing spend has been against the budget and put a halt on anything which is outside the plan.

Or after consideration, you may feel you need to spend more due to market conditions and competitor activity and adjust the budget accordingly. But it is always better to do this knowingly, rather than find out when it is too late to backtrack.

The point is, you have looked at it and considered it in terms of risk and reward on a regular basis. You can trim anything which turns out to be unproven or unnecessary.

Marketing items with unjustifiable expenditure could include local trade exhibitions, directory entries and advertising, trade association fees, industry magazine advertising, and even supporting local charities, to name but a few. Usually, activities like these are sold one-to-one; the business gets an invoice from a telesales executive. Each deal costs relatively little compared with the whole budget. But before you know where you are, the annual budget is overspent by 25%. You had no idea until it was too late to cancel.

4.5 IT Systems and Support

The next category for expense creep is anything to do with IT hardware and software. There is no doubt that you can set an annual budget at the beginning of the year and think all is sorted. Unless you monitor things closely, though, new machines begin to appear in the office, requiring updated licences and more IT support. Innovations to do with remote use of such systems by employees will inevitably mean more contracted costs down the line. If you have a high turnover of people than expected, you will need to account for training them and supporting any gaps in competence with expensive freelancers or additional software amendments.

All this is to simply make the point that unless you review your costs and sales regularly, your business is unlikely to come in under budget or 'on plan'.

Thinking long term, a prospective buyer will also want to know that such changes are constantly under review. They can trust your numbers when you make predictions. If not, it's a great excuse for the buyer to mark down the price or push more of the price into a future earnout formula (more about this in Chapter 8).

4.6 What about Your Customers' Financial Profile?

Many small businesses trade month by month. They tend to value their success by how much money they have in the bank account and how many customers or clients they have. But a prospective buyer will want to see some evidence of stability in the customer base. In broad terms, this means evidence that your larger customers have an ongoing contract with you, that they are profitable for you, and that not all your eggs are in one basket.

Typically, a small business will have two or three larger customers and a tail of many small ones. The problems in getting a good price for your business will revolve around how 'safe' the big customers are in terms of financial commitment and whether the smaller ones are even worth having at all.

If you have, say, just two large customers, the buyer will want to see long-term contracts so that the business does not just evaporate as soon as it is bought if one of them cancels. If your industry operates without contracts as such, you should keep a detailed record of how much and when the large customers make their purchases so that you can 'prove' to a buyer that there is an established buying pattern, even if there are no formal contracts.

Smaller customers are still good if it can be shown that some of the profitable ones become major customers at some future date and so help the business grow. Or that they make repeat orders without having to sell to them again. Keeping good records will help you prove this, if asked.

At any time, you should be able to look up the profitability of every client so you can see what leeway there is to offer discounts or add extra support in order to secure a higher sales total for the year. If you don't know, you often end up giving big discounts to smaller, older customers, because you know them personally. You tend to forget about the opportunities with more recent clients to do more for them.

In an ideal world, you will want to have, say, five large customers who may represent 75% of your sales, with the smaller tail of ad hoc customers taking up the final 25%. By tracking what percentage of your sales are the bigger clients, you can allocate more resources to them and less to the smaller customers. It may be that you need to stop servicing some of the smaller customers as they take up a disproportionate amount of time when viewed from a profit viewpoint.

It is very easy to be fiercely loyal to your first few customers and to continue to spend time with them, almost regardless of their value to the business, as the years go by. You realise that you are wining and dining the smallest contributors to your profits and ignoring the bigger clients who have come along in the meantime. It's easily done because they are 'old friends'. It is a very comfortable way to spend a lunchtime, for sure. Meanwhile, you are neglecting the bigger and better opportunities because you are simply not available to do the legwork and hand-holding that new customers need and often expect.

In the same way, you should be looking at your clients in terms of market sector to ensure you are not beholden to just one part of the economy. It's great to be in automotive when the automotive sector is doing well. But when it isn't, your business may be in jeopardy. By tracking what part of the market your customers are from, you can balance up the risk by going for other market sectors. A balanced spread of customers across the economy is a better proposition for an eventual buyer than a small business that only operates in one niche area.

One other issue to bear in mind is whether any of your clients require you to work exclusively for them in their sector for reasons of product confidentiality. This is all fine if they are prepared to pay you a premium for only dealing with them in that sector. If not, you may be better advised to decline the customer so that you can work for more than one in the same sector.

In my experience, the financial services sector is unusual in its approach to this issue. They *prefer* you to have worked in their sector before because they do not need to explain to you the dynamics of their marketplace or some of their more unusual business terminology.

To some extent, the pharmaceutical sector is similar, provided you are not also working specifically for their direct competitor's new product. These are details you need to establish at the very beginning of a potential relationship for when, eventually, procurement provides the paperwork for you to start billing them.

4.7 Premises, Leases, and Site Costs

When you come to sell, premises often come up as a deal-breaker, depending on your lease terms. But it also represents a fixed cost in your budget which comes around every month. It is impossible to reduce these ongoing costs, unless you decide to move.

If the cost of being on a site is significant, the renewal terms of a lease need careful consideration, as it is all too easy simply to get your legal firm to do it on your behalf. Then later you realise you have committed yourself to a long-term financial arrangement you did not want.

If you are in a growth phase and the economy looks good for the foreseeable future, then a long-term lease is attractive, say, five years. But build in a break clause, say, after two or three years, if you can, so that you can upsize or downsize, depending on the market. If you don't do this, you may find yourself committed to much more space than you need, with no way to reduce the fixed cost should times get tough.

Equally, if you have taken on more staff, you may then have to source another site to house them, with all the problems of having two teams to manage. In a positive commercial market, many landlords will try to go for the longest term with no break clauses if they know there is sufficient demand. In a negative market, you should be able to get some concessions from the landlord, who will be keen to make his or her properties pay their way rather than stand empty.

One issue to watch out for is the charge for regular maintenance, which is usually in addition to the rent and may include all fixtures and fittings, particularly air-conditioning, for example, which is expensive to fix if it goes wrong. Don't forget items such as elevator maintenance if you have leased space in an office block, your share of the gardens outside the office, and even reasonable upkeep of the internal and external décor.

Many leases require you to restore the space to the condition it was in when you moved in. This may be more than just a few tins of magnolia paint. If you decided to erect some wall panels, say, to create more meeting rooms, they may need to be dismantled before you leave, at your expense, if the landlord does not want them. Chances are, you will not be able to use the panels in your new premises. This is all money lost which you probably did not budget for.

The upside of the post-Covid era is that many employees are not averse to working from home. It may be that you could consider operating from smaller premises in the future, with enough on-site space for key people who need to consult with each other regularly. Phone-based team members may prefer to work regularly from home nowadays, provided they have the right software and an Internet connection that is reliable.

If you are responsible for making or selling physical things as a small business to customers or clients, you may not be able to avoid having a site to work in. But you need to remain alert to changes in government or local legislation regarding waste disposal and on-site facilities for team members.

With the current trend towards responsible sustainability, dealing with toxic waste can be a significant number in the budget, especially if you change your processes and find you have more waste than you used to have. Simply having adequate space to store waste rather than have to get rid of it immediately can be a challenge if you have already committed to a smaller site for five years.

4.8 Professional Costs

Although professional costs may be relatively small, annually, they are still a fixed cost you can do little about once they are agreed at the beginning of the financial cycle. To reduce the risk of these costs getting out of control, you need to clearly define what you want the professional to do and how involved you want them to be. Professional costs usually include financial accounting, legal and human resources. Let's look briefly at financial services.

4.9 Financial Reports and Auditing

Every business needs to report its activities to local or national revenue offices to pay or mitigate taxes. This is normally completed after the financial year end. It's a historic task in the main which provides a snapshot of how things went. Too many small business owners see this task as tiresome, time-heavy, and pointless in that it takes the team away from making more profits for the current year. Many small businesses delay filing their accounts as they are not required to pay any taxes until they are filed, a cost which can be delayed. They congratulate themselves on their business acumen.

The opposite is true. A good accountant will drill down into the detail of what you have been doing, point out where you have wasted money, say how to be more efficient with your processes, and provide some pointers for the current year about how to do things more profitably.

Your annual or quarterly report is a gold mine of new ideas for your business which you can only benefit from. As the financial expert is usually not involved day-to-day with operations, it becomes much easier for them to see where things are going wrong. This is especially true when they bring their knowledge of what other clients do to the table. That way, you benefit from not having to try out new things which may or may not have any commercial value.

For example, if your product or service margins are unusually low when compared with similar businesses, the accountant can identify why that might be and suggest ways to save on costs. Often, these days, being pointed in the direction of some new software, such as an app, may seem like a small suggestion. But in reality, it could save you thousands over a full year.

Being comfortable with the way you have always done things financially is a big red flag. Open yourself up to new suggestions, especially in this traditionally dry and boring area. You will be surprised by the results. Delaying the annual financial review just means you will be slow to make any meaningful improvements to profitability for the future.

I often get asked when is the best time to employ a financial professional in the business itself, rather than to simply do it at the year end. My response has always been the same. The best time is a year earlier than you did it. In other words, in-house financial people not only take you to task about wasting money or overspending every day but also do it in the full knowledge of how your business operates in the real world. Even a small business can afford an unqualified financial administrator who will be able to streamline your cash position so that you know how much you have at any time and when you can afford to spend some of it.

Think of it in terms of running a fleet of trucks. It's cheaper, and more effective, to have the mechanic on-site than to wait for breakdowns and hope your outsourced mechanic is free to sort the problem as and when it happens. The longer your trucks are off the road, the more money you are losing.

4.10 Legal Support Costs

Not every business needs legal support all the time. In fact, legal services are often a distress purchase which only comes up when things go wrong.

The most common instance is employer legislation when it comes to disciplining or letting team members go. Employee relations are easy for a small business owner to get wrong, not always being fully aware of changes to recent employee law. The effects of bad people management can run into many thousands in costs and last several months, if not years, in some cases. It's always better to have an ongoing relationship with a people resources legal firm to be on hand to provide good advice as and when things happen. Once you have made the error, they are very difficult and expensive to undo.

The second most likely need for legal help is when things go wrong with customers, either in delivery or in payment. This will no doubt revolve around the contract and its terms, if indeed there are any.

All new orders or customers need a good commercial contract. Professional customers and clients expect it. As long as
they are 'standard industry practice', there should be no issue.
The problems begin when you fail to supply a contract and
rely on telephone calls or emails. Although it may seem overly
formal, contracts for every job or service should be standard to
avoid a disproportionate amount of time dealing with customer complaints or misunderstandings.

The third most obvious need for legal advice is when
you are buying a new business or selling your own. This
should never be done on a handshake or an exchange of
emails. You may love your business buddy to bits, but when
you or they do not deliver what was promised, you will
have no way to get your money back or put things right.
Getting good commercial advice, which includes a formal
sale or purchase contract and a well-thought-through list of
warranties – a list of things the purchase price covers and
does not cover – is essential for your peace of mind once
any deal is done. Nobody wants to be taking people to court
for non-delivery with all the stress and cost of doing so.
Litigation simply to recover lost costs or bad debts can be
very expensive.

4.11 Investing Surplus Cash

The impression you get from most of the media is that small
businesses are always strapped for cash and constantly have
no ready resources to hand. It all depends on what business
sector you work in. It is not unusual for relatively small businesses to be holding hundreds of thousands in cash from
clients who have paid deposits or, in some cases, paid upfront
for services not yet delivered. The key thing to remember
is that this money is not yours. It may as well be in a bank,
because you will have to give it back at some stage, less your

profit margin. So you need to be careful about treating this surplus cash as 'yours'.

That said, there are opportunities to invest this dead money for the benefit of your business. When interest rates are historically high, there are many fixed-rate or overnight banking accounts which make a lot of sense and can deliver a small margin of financial profit, depending on the amount invested. Most banks offer such a service to small businesses specifically to deal with surplus cash.

But avoid tying up customer or client money in speculative investments. You will need the principal amount back at some time to service the client's needs. Putting it into stocks to make a quick buck is not recommended as, statistically speaking, stocks are long-term investments and should not be gambled with for short-term gain. After all, it's not actually yours to gamble with in the first place.

4.12 Lack of Planning

Now that you have the money sorted, we need to bring out the elephant in the room for most small businesses: the lack of planning. Many entrepreneurs excuse their lack of planning by claiming to rely on their natural flair and business know-how. That may be true for some special individuals, but for ordinary people like you and me, doing a plan means thinking about what might go wrong in the future, not just hoping everything will be okay.

KEY LEARNINGS

- Keep track of your cash at all times; don't just hope for the best.
- Adding extra people is easily done, but do you really need them all?

- Marketing budgets always creep upwards, so check them every month.
- IT is the great hidden cost, but does it always deliver added value?
- Old clients are not always the best clients in the long run.
- Financial expertise is always worth the money; get it on board earlier rather than later.
- If you are buying or selling a business, get proper legal advice.

Note

1 H. L. Mencken, "*A Mencken Chrestomathy*", Random House, 1949.

Chapter 5

Failing to Plan Is Planning to Fail

Although I suggested in my introduction that 'things just happen', this is not strictly true. If I could only offer one piece of advice to a budding business owner, it would be to make a plan. It may be a poor one or a brilliant one, but at least you would have what 90% of SMEs don't usually have: something to measure yourself against.

5.1 Write Down Your Strategy

Small business owners often say they don't need a strategy because that's what big businesses do. You don't have millions of customers and thousands of team members. The very word *strategy* puts people off doing one. But it just means thinking about what you are doing, preferably before you do it.

Originally, the Greek word *strategos* meant a 'military general'. In other words, it's the way a general sets up his men to win a battle. It's the starting point for action.

Strategy these days is just a short word in business for 'What do you do/sell, who wants it, and will anyone pay

 DOI: 10.4324/9781003532118-6

enough for it so you can make a profit?' When you investigate
the strategies of big businesses, you often find a mission or
vision statement on their website. This is an attempt to encap-
sulate what they are all about in a simple, telling phrase that
everyone can understand, especially their own team members.

Here are some examples (they often change, because the
market changes every quarter):

Nike: *To be the number one athletic brand in the world.*
Pfizer: *We will become the world's most valued company
to patients, customers, colleagues, investors, business
partners, and the communities where we work and live.*
Volkswagen Group: *We want to be the world's most
successful and fascinating automobile manufacturer and
the leading light when it comes to sustainability.*

These phrases are very inspiring. They are designed in such
a way to mean something to all the many thousands of team
members. Because they are already global organisations with
enormous amounts of financial support, they can afford to talk
about leading the world in their particular field. But you get
the point. The statement sets out their plan, how they are set
up as a business, or their strategy.

You may say, 'Easier said than done'. But in order to
achieve the strategy, every word of the statement needs to
be supported by plans that collectively will deliver the big
ambition.

For example, in the Pfizer mission statement, they say
they want to be 'the world's most valued company'. They will
have had to define what they mean by *value* – Stock price?
Regarded by customers as 'the best'? Loved by staff? Loved by
users such as the medical profession? Each of these objectives
needs a clear plan to be seen as 'the most valued' and a mea-
surement mechanism by which they can see if they are indeed
the 'most valued'.

How does this apply to a small, local business that simply wants to get established and pay its way? The language may change, but the value of having a main purpose that everyone can understand is the same as it is for large organisations.

For example:

Retail owner: Stock groceries people want to buy from a place that customers enjoy coming to.

Plumber: Provide any kind of maintenance and emergency plumbing within 48 hours of enquiry.

Hairdresser: Be the go-to salon for local people and families.

Advertising agency: To be known as the most creative and business-like agency in our client sectors.

It is clear from these examples that some work needs to be done to make sure the 'strategy' can be delivered on a regular basis. You may say, 'Doesn't every small business want to do these things?' Sure. But how many deliver the promise? At the end of each month, you could return to the strategy and measure your activity against what you set out to achieve. The retail owner could track repeat customers through a loyalty scheme to see if, indeed, they do return and what they thought of the shopping experience. The plumber could easily measure the average timings of their response to calls. The hairdresser could simply record how many people from the same family visit for regular hair care, and so on. The advertising agency could enter and record all awards and client testimonials and play it back in their self-promotion. It's always good to have a point of difference for customers if you work in a sector that is commonplace and, therefore, very competitive.

Without doing much or, indeed, any formal research, it is easy to settle on a customer offer that people find attractive, such as responding quickly to plumbing queries. The hard bit is achieving it on a regular basis. Making the strategy work can only be done through action or tactics. Because strategy is just the way you set things up. You haven't actually done anything yet. Tactics are what really matter for a small business as the weeks and months go by.

Tactics are what you do rather than just what you talk about. Tactics come after the plan and define how you go about achieving the plan at the practical level. *Tactics* also derives from Ancient Greek which originally meant how the general moves his troops and resources around to win the battle *during* the battle. It's a dynamic thing, involving action and responding to what happens rather than something discussed or laid out in a document beforehand, never to be spoken about again.

So you are happy with your strategy and think you have a point of difference that customers will be happy with or at least be happy enough to allow you to make a margin on your prices. The practical things you then do, *the tactics*, to deliver the strategy statement are what your business does on a daily basis that separates you from your direct competitors.

From the earlier examples, these tactics could include:

■ A comfortable place to sit/relax for customers
■ Instant callback routine for emergency services, possibly outsourced
■ Activities for children while the adults are serviced
■ Regular promotions about popular items
■ Easy parking facilities
■ Loyalty scheme for regular customers
■ Additional but related services, such as cosmetics or general home maintenance

All these add-ons to the basic service may turn out to be the main reason customers return or, indeed, pay a premium locally, rather than travel to a more distant but less-expensive service provider. But they need to be planned for so as not to disappoint. If calling back immediately is a big point of difference for a plumber, you need to set up a reliable system and deliver the service, even when you think it is costing you money, such as during weekends or public holidays.

Often, the point of difference is a side issue to your specific service, and you may have to employ specialists in those areas to provide what is required. You will certainly need to budget for it. You should also be brave enough to withdraw the offer if it turns out no one values it. What sounded like a good idea in the strategy may turn out to be a costly idea in the real world of tactics. Trying things out is what a successful entrepreneur does.

5.2 Example of Tactical Change

Here's an example. I recently enjoyed a short cruise from the UK to the Netherlands. The clientele was mostly over 50, but not all. There were some toddlers and babies, presumably of parents who could not be separated from their small children. On one of the upper decks, there was also a crèche – and that made sense because of the minority client profile. Next to the crèche was an area branded *The Teenzone*. It was empty, was locked up, and looked uncared for. I never saw any teenagers during the entire four days. But I could well imagine why the designers thought it might be a good idea at the planning stage, if they were also creating a crèche. It wasn't.

You need to be brave enough to stop offering benefits that no one wants, even though you may have been doing it for years. It is costing you money and maintenance resources which could certainly be used elsewhere.

5.3 Do a Budget and Review It Regularly

Assuming you are happy with your main strategy and can afford the tactics you are going to use to support that strategy, you need to cost it all out. Very few small businesses do an annual budget, otherwise known as a financial plan. In fact, most do not know if they are going to make a profit for any particular period until the accountant does the numbers at the end of the year. If they make a large profit, the owner is usually very surprised. Being surprised is no way to run a business. As many owners will tell you, they can cope with bad news and good news, but surprising news is very difficult to handle.

Doing an annual budget, split into periods, ideally monthly, rather than quarterly, not only provides peace of mind when sales may not go according to plan but also highlights any wastage in terms of things you don't need to keep paying for because you can see they don't deliver any benefit. It's better to know that during the year rather than some months after the end of the period, when there's nothing you can do to change it. Losses are things that can be changed as you go along, rather than simply accept, long after the horse has bolted.

The usual defence against not having an annual or interim budget is that experienced entrepreneurs can tell from their sales turnover whether they are making a profit. To some extent, this is true. If you have one million in cash in your current account, you may think that reviewing a budget is a waste of time as you know your costs are around, say, 800,000. What such an analysis doesn't show is what purchase taxes need to be paid, for example, or other big costs that you had forgotten about when you sell more than you thought you would.

This becomes more critical if there is a dip in the economy that no one saw or a change in legislation that may be vital to your service. Cash in the bank may still be a lot when compared with a household budget. But it soon goes when inspectors call and fines are issued, not to mention all the sudden price increases by suppliers during a downturn.

Budgets allow you to see where you are at any time and give you time to react, either by cutting back on costs or investing in better processes to deliver things less expensively. If you simply don't know what your ongoing costs are, how will you be ready to pay for them when the time comes?

5.4 Don't Sweat the Small Stuff

A plan helps you see what is important and what really makes little difference to the success of the business. Sometimes, just looking at the budget puts things in perspective.

Salespeople expenses often come up as major concerns. But are they really in the context of the entire year's budget? It can be very annoying for operational team members in a small business to hear about sales executives' hospitality expenses, such as bar bills, golf fees, or in their opinion, travel costs which far exceed their own domestic expenses. This is a major misunderstanding about the difference between what people pay for out of earned income and what businesses must pay out before they can make profits. The two are not related.

5.5 Sales Team Expenses

No average team member would willingly pay for business class seats on a plane if there was a cheaper version available or even a cheaper carrier. But often, business people need to be at a certain place by a certain time, and securing that travel slot usually costs more than standard cattle class. This is not to say that, as the owner of the business, you might question why the salesperson took a business class flight when there was a perfectly reasonable and less-expensive alternative. Or you may wonder why your person ended up paying for all the drinks for a client night out when it could have been shared between the other hosts or even with the client. This is all about tactical management of costs and tweaking the way you do things to get a slightly better result for the business.

In the overall budget, sales expenses may be less than, say, 1% of total sales turnover, and as long as they stay within that parameter, it's better to have a happy sales team member who can work on the journey and arrive refreshed for that important meeting rather than someone who is tired, ill-prepared, and perhaps anxious about the journey back without the flexibility of business class fares.

5.6 Maintenance Costs Are Not 'Strategic'

Another example could be the costs of cleaning and maintaining the office or premises. Sure, you may be able to get another firm to charge less or only do the job every third or fourth day. But what message does this give your team members, who, at the very least, expect to work in a clean and tidy environment in order to give their very best shot at the day's tasks? You may have saved a small amount over the year by choosing the least-expensive supplier, but what you don't want are resentful employees who will soon tire of having to tidy their working environment two or three times a week simply so that 'management' can make a small and insignificant saving.

5.7 Planning Means Concentrating on the Important Stuff

By having a budget that the senior team have helped you put together and agreed, it is very easy to see what costs a lot each month and what does not. Here are some big-ticket items from any annual budget that deserve to be discussed at the monthly planning meeting:

■ Annual staff costs
■ Premises
■ Major suppliers
■ IT changes

5.8 Annual Team Remuneration

Your team costs could easily be 50% or more of your overall costs for the year, so they should be regularly reviewed. Not to cut them but simply to see if you were right when you put the plan together. When you are growing and perhaps selling more than you expected to, it is likely you will need more people to do the work. But it's your job to ensure that additional costs are controlled from the centre.

If you simply allow operational managers to take on new people as and when they feel they need to, your costs will rise unchecked as every manager could do with more people – it's a given fact of business life, especially if you are growing.

It's okay to add more people than were in the budget, provided someone has calculated that you will have more sales to cover their costs. Because many businesses are cyclical, sales don't come in neatly and proportionately quarter by quarter; it may be that your busy times only come, say, twice a year. By taking on more staff to handle the peaks comfortably, you will end up with idle hands in the not-so-busy period, but their costs will still be there. The senior team need to monitor these variations on a regular basis so you don't end up with the costs of a big team and losses from less sales.

5.9 Premises Costs Need Reviewing All the Time

Premises are relatively predictable, so you may think there is not much to worry about on a regular basis. But most leases provide for an opportunity to renegotiate at least every two years. That means you should at least have the discussion about whether you are going to stay where you are or downsize (or even upsize) to match the expected work. It's too late to moan about unnecessary overheads the month after you have just signed up to 'five more years' in the same premises with an even higher rental than before.

5.10 Be Strategic about 'Comfortable' Suppliers

Knowing who your major suppliers are can make a significant difference to your profits if you can negotiate better deals on the back of higher-than-expected sales. Small businesses often become comfortable with their early-years partners as they will have offered good solutions at a critical time. But things change. New suppliers appear, and there could be significant technical and cost advantages of thinking about changing suppliers. Inevitably, it will be uncomfortable as the new supplier will need to adjust to your needs. But it's even more uncomfortable to be with a supplier for ten years only to discover that what they now offer is out-of-date and more expensive than others.

5.11 IT, Be Alert to Technology Changes

Improvements in business technology have often been introduced more quickly than expected in recent years. Your costs for internal communication, telephones, tracking systems, and warehousing, for example, have come down significantly. The rise of 'apps' in all walks of life has improved service and communication levels beyond recognition. In some cases, even the office you work in may be less important than it used to be. Customers and clients now have the option to meet online rather than travel to potential suppliers. There are arguments on both sides as to which is best.

But it's a given that there may be a number of manual processes you go through to deliver your product or service to customers which could more easily be done through automation. Software is improving all the time, driven by mobile phone technology and data held remotely rather than sitting in someone's computer at a fixed location.

The chances are that your IT costs will have increased beyond what you will have been paying, say, five years ago. But you will be offering a quicker, more reliable, better-quality product or service. This is just one reason you need to review IT costs against the plan on a regular basis to see what's out there in terms of reliability and speed. If you don't do it, your nearest competitor will. It does not take long to be perceived as 'old-fashioned', and no amount of home-spun friendliness will make up for simply being out of touch. As a result, you will no longer be the first choice anymore for repeat purchasers or users.

5.12 How Often Should You Replan, and How?

If you are reviewing your plan on a tactical level every month or quarter, you will be changing things as you go along. But there does come a time when you start to think whether you need a major overhaul of some of the things you are doing which may take more time than a month's quick fix. If you have changed a particular process five or six times, it may be a good idea to assess whether what you want could be better achieved by a completely new solution, if one exists. A new approach will probably need time to implement and cost more than you currently have in the budget. Rather than just forget about making the improvement because of the cost, you could park it for more discussion in the 'annual review'.

5.13 A Once-a-Year Away Day for Team Members

It's good to review everything you are doing, if only to remind yourself what business you are in, despite all the tactical changes that happen during the year. But even the best senior team don't have all the answers. Before you disappear off to your spa hotel into your secret room with your senior team, you should ask ordinary team members what issues, if any, they have about the way you do things. The best strategy comes from the best research. Reviewing your strategic plan is a two-stage process.

5.14 Team Members Get-Together

Get all the end year numbers together, put them in an easy-to-understand visual format, and run a team day, preferably off-site. Half the day should be reviewing the business, with the other half reserved for fun activities and some good food. What usually happens is that most team members say very little, as this will probably be the first time they have seen the confidential business numbers. They will be unsure what to make of them as they won't know what's normal and what isn't. But they will all be very grateful to be treated like adults in a joint enterprise, even if they don't own the business themselves. If you have created an atmosphere of open discussion, you will get some very valuable feedback on the operational issues of the business. As most senior people do not handle the day-to-day delivery, it is often very revealing how things are viewed at the operational end of the business and what issues they must deal with.

In essence, this is a research day for the business where lots is discussed but no promises are made, as the cost of any seemingly obvious improvement may simply not be possible without more investment. Getting extra cash for developing the business is a whole other ball game. Be careful not to promise implementing any process changes or improvements at the meeting, as costs are not always immediately obvious or even knowable. There's nothing worse for the senior team than promising to do something and then not doing it, with no reasons given as to why not.

5.15 Planning Day for Senior Staff, Off-Site

Armed with direct feedback from the business, give yourself enough time to cost out a few innovations and then hold your annual strategy review. It sounds very grand, but if you go off-site, it gives the senior team the chance to go back to basics, review the numbers in detail, think about any major changes you may wish to make, and agree on the budget in principle for the following year. Get everyone to turn their cell phones off for the main sessions. There is nothing so important right now as hearing what people have to say.

One of the main talking points should be profit margins. I've never had a business yet where the profit margins could not be improved by examining incoming costs and outgoing prices. It may be the opportunity to raise your prices, bearing in mind inflation and perhaps what competitors are charging too. Too many small businesses are afraid to raise their prices for fear of losing long-standing customers. Naturally, all businesses are conscious of the wider economic environment. But if they fail to keep up with the market and inflation, they will erode their profits so much that the business is no longer viable – then everyone loses their job.

An often-forgotten agenda item is your people. Items for discussion should include keeping pay and benefits competitive, thinking about the career progression of key team members, and potential new recruits for a changing business. It makes for a happier ship if management are the ones to push these improvements through rather than wait for team members to complain or threaten to leave. It's all about being a great place to work, however lowly or local you may think your business is. If people are happy, they stay and continue to do a good job for you. If they leave, new recruits will be expensive to find and be less effective than experienced team members.

5.16 Planning for a Better Future

If you are doing all these things, profits will follow, as will the value of the entire enterprise. The big question is what to do with these profits. Put them in the bank and earn next to nothing on them? Or invest in the future? As you will discover in Chapter 9, my final chapter, selling your business or businesses over the years can deliver ×20 more earnings power than simply being an employee.

So if you have a good few years of growth, is buying another business the way forward rather than just reinvesting any spare cash into your first and only enterprise?

KEY LEARNINGS

- Do a strategy even if it is pretty obvious; you will learn a lot just thinking about what it might be.
- Decide on your tactics: What are you going to do differently this time around?
- Review your budget regularly, but don't sweat the small stuff too much.
- Your team costs are going to be your largest expense, so keep an eye on them.
- Ask your senior team what they think before you write out your plan.
- An away day out of the workplace for everyone will help you make a plan better.

Chapter 6

Grow Gradually, Acquire, or Sell?

Business owners are naturally impatient to get things done. If they weren't, they would soon go out of business. Of the many ways to grow a business, simply continuing to do what you do is fine for some business owners. The merits are many; no sudden changes, you become more efficient with your processes, and your team become experts, if you manage to hold on to them. If you are lucky, you get to manage people rather than do all the work yourself. Life becomes financially predictable. You may even get to take time away from the business on a pre-planned basis. No more panics, cell phone calls by the pool, or last-minute solutions to find.

But what if government legislation changes and impacts your major product? Or you lose those two or three big customers you rely on? Or your best people leave, for whatever reason?

Suddenly, you've got to begin again. Big changes could set you back years, if not decades, just when you thought you had to keep on doing what you do until you retire. It can all get very slow and repetitive when you need to begin again.

DOI: 10.4324/9781003532118-7

What's worse, you know in detail how much effort it has taken to get to where you are today. Will you be up for doing it all one more time?

The other downside from just doing what you do is that it may not be delivering the growth that you wanted or expected fast enough. Retirement may seem very far away when you are in your 40s or 50s, but being able to stop working full-time exactly when you want is just not going to happen. Even if you sell your business for a good sum, you will probably be asked to stay on for a year or two to 'bed it down' for the new owner. They are unlikely to have someone just like you waiting in the wings.

The dream of finding a friendly buyer who will pay you 100% cash up front and politely ask you to step aside on deal day rarely happens. As you will see in Chapter 8, selling your business at the end of your career is more like a transition than a single point in time.

Should you just keep on keeping on? Or should you acquire another business to get things moving more quickly? Or even sell some part of your business which may be dragging the entire business or service offering down?

Adding more sales from the existing team may simply not be possible. If it were, you would be doing it anyway. There comes a point with every business where you hit capacity in terms of skills or simply the available market. No amount of huffing and puffing is going to change that. The obvious answer is to buy another business with your current profits.

6.1 Opportunities to Grow Faster

It may not be in your plan, but sometimes businesses come to you, rather than you having to go out looking for one. In fact, the first time you ever need to consider selling up is probably when someone makes an unexpected offer for it.

There are many ways you can be challenged to acquire a new business, even if you are perfectly happy with the way things are. The most obvious is the unsolicited approach from a company broker or a financial professional. This may be in the guise of a cryptic email asking you to contact an unknown person about a confidential business matter. A quick online search will reveal that they represent a brokerage that buys and sells other businesses. Your business has reached the top of their pile when it comes to being identified as a potential target for one of their clients.

This type of approach, although flattering, is rarely as personalised as it looks. Most company brokers mail regularly thousands of prospects in the hope that, say, 1% or 2% will express an interest. This is normal in B2B marketing. It does no harm to respond if you are genuinely seeking to expand your business through acquisition. But be prepared to kiss a lot of frogs before finding a suitable partner. It is very unlikely that an unsolicited approach will tick all your boxes when it comes to finding a new business to acquire yours.

It may be, of course, that you will find a suitable acquisition on their website, where they list other businesses for sale. But often they do not list all their clients. Selling a business is a highly confidential issue, especially when it comes to trust. They don't want to be giving away financial details publicly to competitors.

After all, what clients would want to begin a new commercial relationship with you if they know that you are looking to sell your business in the near future? They may even have concerns if they know you, yourself, are looking to buy another business. Cash is always important when it comes to assessing a supplier's creditworthiness. The last thing a client wants is to engage with a new business who might be about to stretch both its finances and its management team with a new venture.

Competitors will be delighted to tell their contacts that you are looking to acquire or be acquired and that they would be best advised to avoid doing business with you for the time being, until things settle down.

6.2 Appointing an Agent to Find a Business to Buy

The flip side of the same coin is to proactively appoint an agent or broker yourself, having briefed them on what you are looking for. This is by far a more convenient way for you to search the market and see what is available at a price which is attractive for you as the buyer. It allows you to make enquiries without giving away your identity from the very beginning.

Professional services don't come for free, of course. Depending on the slickness of the sales approach, you may be asked to pay a substantial upfront fee to cover 'marketing' plus further fees down the line as and when buyers are made aware of your interest in any acquisition. There will be stage payments based on how serious the offers are.

At the end of the process, you should expect to pay a substantial percentage fee to the broker for a successful completion. This could easily be as much as, if not more than, you may have to pay for legal advice on the sale contract, so be warned.

When you add up all the fees, consultancy fees, and costs, it would not be unreasonable to discover that you will pay between 5% and 10% of the eventual purchase cost to the agents and legal professionals simply to get the job done.

So whatever the price you have in your mind to acquire a new business, you need to consider the transaction costs as extra. Just like buying or selling your home.

6.3 Appointing an Agent to Sell Your Own Business

The story is much the same when it comes to selling your own business. There will be an initial confirmation fee, then probably an ongoing monthly fee to cover their research and marketing time, stage payments for progressing any serious deals, and finally, a success fee, which may be, say, 3% and 5% or more of the eventual sale price. The argument here is that they are incentivised to get the highest sales price they can for your 'once-in-a-lifetime' transaction. In theory, their fee comes out of the higher price they have been able to get for you.

6.4 Watch Out for the Small Print

You will be asked to sign a contract with the broker which obliges you to pay all the fees mentioned whether or not you are still using them to broker your deal. It is not uncommon for a seller to get very close to signing off on a deal, only to find there has been a change of heart at the last minute and the deal is off. That contact may then return to you privately a few years down the line and say the deal may be back on again. Even if you are no longer dealing with the original broker, they will still press for the success fees based on the fact that they introduced you originally and, without them, you would not have made the contact, even if it is years later.

You may have decided by then to use a new broker for the revitalised sale possibility. Their contract probably says the same thing. So you could end up, in theory, paying two lots of fees to two separate brokers for buying just one entity.

One sensible way forward is to exclude certain target companies at the outset from the deal, or parts of it, to ensure you don't pay brokers twice. It could be you have some ideal candidates from your own contacts in business or previous dealings and conversations and would prefer to make contact yourself, without an intermediary.

Clearly, if there is work to be done, such as re-establishing contact or holding initial conversations or framing the deal which you would rather not do, then the broker needs to be paid for their time.

6.5 What Sort of Acquisition Works Best?

It goes without saying that a successful acquisition to your benefit is usually a business that you understand and can add value to.

Often, it is complementary to the things you do, such as adding a new type of client, a new service, or allows you to make cost savings which you could not do without it. It is not enough to just look at the bottom line and think, 'That's better than I can do. I'll buy it'.

You have to be able to add value to what it does or be confident enough in your management skills that you can do a better job than the current owner or team.

Never underestimate the ability of the target management team or, indeed, the individual who runs it. Often, what makes for a successful organisation comes from the top, even if they no longer speak to the customers or get involved on a daily basis. Loyalty counts for a lot in small businesses. There is much know-how and ability in the second tier of operations which are easy to ignore until you find yourself having to replicate or do things better than the old boss.

The best acquisitions are those which can integrate easily into your current framework and who share your views about how to run things and the markets they work best in. For example, if you manufacture shoes and are pretty good at it, it makes no sense to acquire a software organisation simply because their margins are better than yours.

With the likelihood that the current owners will leave the acquired business within a year, or sometimes less, you will not have the industry skills or contacts to replace them. What's worse, you may try to shoehorn them into a manufacturing way of working, because it's what you know, and end up with a demoralised senior team who spend their first year looking for other employment.

6.6 Will It Be Successful?

You need to be careful to set some parameters for success that mean something to your acquired business. Profits are not enough, although it could be one measure. Being acquired by another business, especially if they are not on-site, can be very unsettling for the team who had no say in who buys it.

Measures for 'success' include retention of key people, maintenance of sales volumes, quality measures for production or service, cooperation between the old and the new teams, cost control improvements, market share, and employee engagement, if you can measure it.

6.7 Selling Off Parts or Letting People Go

One aspect of acquiring a new business may well be to then discard some of the resources they currently have, either because you already have them or they are simply not paying their way anymore in the new set-up.

It is very hard to say immediately what works well and what does not on the day you acquire a new organisation. It can take a year or more to work out which parts of what you have bought are efficient and which are treading water. Resist the urge to go in all guns blazing in the first few months in an attempt to make some efficiency savings. It may not be obvious that some of the ways the acquired organisation does things turn out to be the best way to do it in practice. Looking in from the outside, you do not see the complexities the business has had to adapt to in the past. So change things at your peril, at least in the first six months of ownership.

6.8 Merging with Another Business

When you acquire an additional business, there is always lots to think about in terms of efficiency. If your business is close by, then having both organisations on the same site makes a lot of sense. You can save on duplicated site costs and, in some cases, duplicated common services, such as administration and finance. It is also much easier to manage in terms of people issues. Solving problems before they become problems is good management practice. But you cannot do it if you are not on-site.

Be careful with an acquired business that has a known and recognised brand in the marketplace. Brands are complicated assets which live in the minds of consumers rather than in the files of the business.

It may feel attractive to simply rebrand the acquired product as your own and feel very good about it. However, customers of the old brand will probably rush out and buy your closest rivals' products in the sudden absence of the established brand. You will have destroyed the value of your acquisition at a stroke.

Using phrases such as 'part of the X organisation/family of services' is a good way to keep the acquired brands in a holding pattern until you have done enough research to convince yourself that changing the brand or letting it die is a good and viable idea.

The smart thing to do would be to maintain the acquired brand and continue as normal, at least as far as the outside world is concerned, until you are sure that any changes you make will increase profitability or efficiency. This process of assessment and improvement could take several months or even years. Rushing to get it done is not a positive move.

Ideally, you need to at least maintain the success of the acquired business and present an impression of 'business as usual' so that you retain as much goodwill and existing customers as possible. In my experience, the best acquisitions are those where the customers are hardly aware there are new owners. But they are pleasantly surprised that soft factors, such as marketing and financial or administration processes, are much improved. They are the real measures of success for any acquired business.

6.9 Integrate . . . or See It Die

An important part of the acquisition plan should be how you intend to integrate the acquired team into the wider organisation.

If the new team is required to work from your existing premises, it is inevitable that you will lose a few team members along the way, as often junior members cannot or will be unwilling to change their domestic travelling routines simply to keep their job.

In addition, it is customary to provide financial assistance for an initial period after the acquisition to help with this transition. No one should be disadvantaged by the takeover. This means, from a budgeting viewpoint, there will be costs in losing people and having to recruit replacements as well as compensatory costs for people who cannot easily commute to the new place of work. It is not unusual to fund commuting costs for up to six months or more to encourage acquired team members to 'give it a go'.

If the new acquisition is staying where it is, these costs do not have to be taken into account. But beware: most team members will feel nervous about what a new owner may do, and despite assurances, they will start to look for other employment opportunities 'just in case'. Part of your merge strategy should be constant reassurance that their jobs are safe, if they are, and that all is well.

Joint introductory meetings with the new owners go a long way to establish trust and professional links between the two teams. Fact-finding discussions and exploring ways to work with each other should be carried out as soon as the ink is dry on the deal. Silence or lack of contact is almost always interpreted as bad news by new team members.

6.10 Minority Shareholdings

It is not unusual to come across like-minded businesses that decide to sell off minority shareholdings in their business, both to bank some profit for the owners and to share in the minority owners' know-how going forward. Eventually, they will want to sell out, but perhaps not just now.

This can be quite a complicated legal arrangement. Senior people, in particular, will be worried about their long-term future in a changing leadership situation and be very unsettled, despite, no doubt, being offered a lucrative package to stay. The acquired directors, who may have pocketed a substantial cash sum from the arrangement, will be feeling less pressure to make things work, even though they will still hold many of the joint shares which are, in theory, still valuable.

The minority shareholders will have new share options, broader management responsibilities, or other attractive benefits to keep growing the business under the new joint ownership arrangements.

The acquiring owners will have given themselves a chance to assess how the acquired organisation is doing and have an option to buy it outright at some future stage when certain financial goals are achieved.

This is all good, if it is the only option open. But it's not ideal. Clear exercise of executive power is important to push along any good business. With this type of deal, it can become very political in terms of claiming success or apportioning blame if things go wrong, as they inevitably will at some stage in certain joint processes.

If taking a minority stake is the only option you have, then so be it. But prepare yourself for a number of problems which there would not be if you owned it outright.

6.11 Selling Up and Starting Again

Serial entrepreneurship normally means selling your main business and then starting a new one again. It could be similar. Or it could be completely different. The principle is that if you have a skill in founding or developing early-stage businesses, it makes sense to use those skills in another business scenario, rather than think you need to keep going with the old business until you retire.

It is probably true to say that some people are better at starting new enterprises than running mature ones. Grown-up businesses need seasoned executives who can bring mature skills from other preferably larger organisations rather than the entrepreneurial flair and risk-taking of being the founder.

For many self-made business owners who have done the job properly over the years by employing senior people to handle all the proper business areas, a mature business provides less of a challenge. The early development skills of finding new clients, setting up premises, and experimenting with the best internal processes are what entrepreneurs are good at.

When a business is functioning to industry standards and success is measured in steady progress and improvement with the minimum of risk, with perhaps half an eye on external shareholders and what they expect, the entrepreneur will want to look elsewhere for job satisfaction.

Nothing is standard in life or business. But in general, it takes 8–10 years to get a new business to maturity without a degree of expensive funding. That means in a working lifespan of, say, 40 years, a serial entrepreneur may well expect to establish and run four or five businesses in their lifetime, plus having a few minority shareholdings along the way, as described earlier.

6.12 Should You Grow Gradually or Acquire?

The safe option may well be to grow organically, making your enterprise bigger and better, while positioning it for future growth. That way, you control all the elements that matter. It's probably why you were successful in the first place. As the leader of the business, you have time to see things develop, learn from mistakes, and watch what's going on in your marketplace. The bigger you get, the more attractive you are to new recruits, who perceive you as a 'market leader' and, therefore, somewhere for them to grow their own careers in.

But this all takes time. If you are in your 30s, perhaps time is something you think you have plenty of. If you are older, you may be thinking 'creating a successful business' is just taking too long for it ever to be worth anything substantial. It's not just about selling up and goin' fishin'. You may have sacrificed a lot of time and effort away from your family and want to see a reward for your input which is not linked to retiring early.

If a business is well-delegated, it doesn't take long to realise you could achieve a lot more, more quickly, if you concentrated on expanding the organisation through acquisition rather than waiting for your current team to catch up with your ambitions.

On balance, acquiring new businesses while running your existing one is by far the quickest route to achieving bigger things and a bigger payout. You can add impressive, additional levels of sales simply by acquiring new services or outlets. You just need to be very careful about having the skills to run the acquired businesses simultaneously and be able to wear many hats in the same working week.

If you are happy to be a generalist, good with people, and commercially aware, then growing through acquisitions can be astonishingly fast. Acquiring a business then becomes another of your skill sets which can be repeated, with good people behind you who are all singing from the same hymn sheet as you.

If, at heart, you are a hands-on type of manager who likes to watch over all the processes of what goes on in a business, it is unlikely you will be able to handle the sheer level of detail required in managing another business at the same time. If this is you, grow organically and plan for sale nearer to your retirement.

6.13 Selling Off Part or All of Your Empire

Naturally, there may come a time when you want to divest yourself of all your businesses. But even though they may now all be part of a single group, legally speaking, it is unlikely a buyer will want all of them just because you happen to own them all.

The final part of the entrepreneur's jigsaw is to recognise that selling off your businesses may require you to let them go one by one over several years.

In my experience, I sold off my main business first, with other parts of the organisation being sold piecemeal over the following years, simply because buyers wanted to purchase something specific, not a 'group' of complementary businesses which just happened to have come along. Over time, I bought minority stakes in smaller business with some of the cash as investments, rather than to manage myself. This has attractions as, arguably, businesses are worth more if you sell off the assets in pieces to the right buyers at different times.

The point is that life is never straightforward. People may think that you start a business in your 30s, grow it for 30 years, sell it to the highest bidder in your 60s, then retire. It rarely happens like that.

As an entrepreneur, you will probably own four or five businesses, with varying degrees of equity, sell two off, acquire three more, then sell them all, except one, by the time you are ready to retire. The process of selling off the last couple may take several years and certainly will not be done and dusted on the very date you may have set yourself to retire.

That's what makes it more interesting than being a corporate executive.

KEY LEARNINGS
■ You can grow organically, but it takes a long time; grow faster by acquiring other businesses.
■ Use corporate brokers to find suitable acquisitions, and let them do the work.
■ Buy something you understand; don't just look at the bottom line.

- Consider the differences between buying a business at another site or getting the new team to work at your site.
- Integrating the acquired team is key to a successful outcome.
- You will probably, eventually, own four or five businesses in your career – is this something you are comfortable with?
- Selling off your businesses when you retire is a process, not a fixed date.

Chapter 7

Gifts, Incentives, Bribery . . . Corruption

At some stage in your business career, someone will ask you for something personal to tip a contract in your favour. If they are a supplier, they may give you something to influence your buying decision. Sometimes it may seem trivial, such as tickets to a sports or hospitality event. It may be an invitation to an expensive restaurant for you and your partner. It may even be a holiday. At other times, it is clear that the supplier, for example, expects to get favourable treatment in return for a personal 'gift' to you and your family.

But at what point do relationship-building, marketing, and promotion slide into systematic bribery and corruption?

As a small business owner, you get the opportunity to set standards both in the products or the services you provide and in the way you go about your business. Your team will copy those standards, whatever they are. They become the unwritten way of doing things. New joiners will not question these unsaid behaviours; they will just accept them as the way you do business with your customers.

DOI: 10.4324/9781003532118-8

But when does a thank-you gift become an incentive to change behaviour corruptly? When does an incentive become a bribe in terms of the legal definition?

Much legal alignment has been done in recent years by Western governments and the organisation *Transparency International* to standardise payments and inducements for large state contracts. Payments to individual foreign ministers, for example, were getting out of hand to the extent that the informal inducements were often worth more than the contracts themselves, especially in international defence procurement and large-scale engineering works.

There now exists an international code of conduct for government departments to follow when placing overseas contracts. This was largely created and promoted by the USA, who became increasingly frustrated by potential national business partners placing export business with the country that provides the most value in inducements rather than based on the merits of the project itself.

7.1 The Law on Bribery

In the UK, the Bribery Act (2012) was made law. For the first time, individual business employees could be sent to prison for breaches when previously it was only the organisation itself which could be taken to court. They usually got acquitted with a fine because they could afford good lawyers – and they could blame rogue staff for any irregularities. You could not send an entire workforce to prison if convicted, so the legislation was largely ineffective.

Nowadays, fraud prevention agencies in the developed world regularly prosecute any clear breaches of the law up to a point. But like most public bodies, they have limited resources and tend to go after high-profile, well-known firms as a deterrent to others in that sector and in the business community generally. In any given year, there are very few convictions under the laws of bribery. But that does not mean small-scale entrepreneurs can do what they like without fear of prosecution.

It has been said by some opinion leaders that not being very corrupt is like not being very pregnant. You are either one thing or the other. There are no shades of difference when it comes to systemic corruption.

7.2 Gifts

What do shady dealings in large-scale public procurement have to do with small local business owners? It's a question of how you conduct your business. It affects who is likely to accept a job offer from you, what suppliers will deal with you, and what clients will give you contracts. On the bottom line, it also affects who might buy your business when the time comes to sell. Any unusual expenses outside client contracts will be picked up during the audit phase of selling any business. At some stage, you will have to explain what those expenses were for.

Reputations can be destroyed overnight if you are unaware of doing anything wrong. Nothing can be hidden from social media these days. It's an unlikely defence to say that no one will find out. They probably already know what you are doing; they are just waiting for the right time to tell other people. Disgruntled ex-team members are usually the first to go public with unsavoury practices.

Let's start with the basics. Are gifts acceptable, and if so, whom can I give them to and, more importantly, why should I?

7.3 Custom and Usage

From the beginnings of commercial life the world over, there has been a tradition of offering gifts without cost to those with the power to supply a product or service. In the good old days, this was seen as a thank-you for providing the opportunity to trade. In some parts of the world, this 'side-gift' became what we recognise today as a commission, usually to a middleman, without whom the trade would not have happened. In many markets, payments to middlemen are standard and still persist, particularly in the developing world. They may even be well-known politicians.

The reason for modern regulation of such 'customs' is that the scale of revenues and their potential distribution has increased so much that it is no longer acceptable to turn a blind eye to these so-called local arrangements. In particular, it has become an issue with low-paid, public-sector employees who, by dint of their role, have a big influence over whom a public administration deals with, commercially speaking, even though they may be living on the minimum wage.

7.4 Regulations about Discretional Gifts

But this also applies to small businesses. Most Western governments now have regulations about business-to-business gifts. Normally, they include what value of gift may be appropriate in any given fiscal year and, crucially, that no future trading relationship is implied. This goes for employer-to-employee relationships too. There is usually a statutory amount for a gift which an employee can receive without tax. Just look up what the limits are and be mindful of them if you are considering a festive or annual gift to other people's team members.

Many businesses provide festive or annual thank-you gifts to key clients. In general, these items probably exceed the statutory limits, but it is up to the recipient to declare them as taxable. This can be nuisance for the recipient, which was never your intention. In many organisations, receiving gifts from suppliers, however well meant, is frowned upon due to the relatively recent constraints of law. You need to check whether gifts are acceptable before you send them to all your clients or customers. One man's thank-you is another man's bribe, especially when you are dealing with international organisations.

Some businesses try to circumvent the law on bribery by offering gifts in kind, rather than as physical items. You may think that entertaining a client to an expensive meal or sports event is perfectly okay and no one will ever know. But most legislation outlines the need to keep a register of who is offered what kind of hospitality, and the employee themselves may have to complete an internal procedural note about accepting any hospitality in order to have a sound legal defence should such gifts be queried at some future date when the supplier contract is completed. More often than not, it is a disgruntled supplier who blows the whistle because they are disappointed that they did not get the contracts they were expecting.

This applies equally to invitations, often in quality venues and hotels, which are without cost to the provider but promoted as an educational exercise. There is nothing wrong with trying to promote your services through a seminar or destination visit. But it needs to be recorded by both parties and be seen to be appropriate. For example, if you have a global product with global suppliers, it is perfectly legitimate to fund an event in, say, Paris as a central logistical hub. The law does not punish businesses for wanting to get to know potential clients better by meeting in person. It's all about being appropriate and reasonable, depending on the contract and where the businesses are located.

If your product is only available in your country and your clients are all nationals of that country, it makes no legal sense to hold an event on the other side of the world. Any judge or ordinary jury member will immediately see this as an inappropriate inducement to place business and will judge your behaviour as the provider accordingly.

All that said, new national legislation about potential bribery has spooked the corporate market so much in recent years that large organisation lawyers have been very cautious about employees accepting anything, even if genuinely offered as a gift or thank-you, as it could be perceived to be bribery.

7.5 Pharmaceutical Ethics

A good example is the pharmaceutical industry. When reps visit surgeries and hospitals to promote new drugs, they no longer supply branded pens, notebooks, or other small promotional items, for fear of falling foul of their own corruption guidelines. Any sensible onlooker would say this is not an example of bribery – it's just marketing. But no one wants to be up in court, being made an example of. Or lose their job because of it!

More seriously, it used to be normal for medical consultants and their partners to be sent all over the world to attend medical congresses, ostensibly to hear about new treatments and techniques. But in reality, they viewed these events as free holidays. This way of working has largely stopped as a direct result of international bribery legislation. Doctors and expert consultants still attend such congresses, but these days the hotels chosen are usually of a standard grade rather than a luxury venue, and partners who may accompany have to pay their own way. These days, the meetings are very much about the content rather than the offer of hospitality.

7.6 Record What Has Been Offered and Accepted

A good way to consider whether your 'gifts policy' contravenes the latest legislation is to think what an ordinary member of the public would think should it ever get to court. A biro pen with your company logo on it, provided as a gift without any reciprocation, is clearly not a bribe. An all-expenses-paid trip to New York with no business educational content whatsoever is clearly corrupt.

The key point is to record what you have offered to whom and make it clear that such an offer is not contingent on that guest making a new contract in your favour in the future. The law makes it very clear that giving something to a client to expect business in the future contravenes the law. You could be prosecuted for such persistent activity if it is your standard way to attract new clients.

7.7 When Does an Incentive Become a Bribe?

It is clear, then, that small-scale promotional items and even appropriate hospitality are not bribes, providing you have not given them to potential clients specifically in return for some direct commercial return. Both parties have been open and honest about the 'gift', and no expectation has been set out, verbally or in writing, about repaying that gift in terms of a favourable contract. We can all argue about the words. In essence, the gift should not be linked to any specific future action by the client. Many organisations, particularly those which are publicly owned, insist on paying for their share of any hospitality being offered to ensure there can be no doubt. This may even apply to complimentary restaurant meals, even if the intention is simply to be hospitable. So far, so good.

But what about employee incentives and trade channel incentives? Surely, these are inducements specifically linked to future commercial behaviour along the lines of 'do this, get that'? That is what an *incentive* is.

7.8 Incentives Are Not Bribes

It is fair to say that legislators struggled with this fine distinction between *incentives* and *bribery*. But there is a clear separation. It's all about levels of secrecy.

When the Bribery Act came into force in the UK, business people worried about whether network marketing to meet new people or to develop a personal relationship would now be criminalised. But what about incentive schemes to build new business partnerships?

As outlined earlier, it was never the intention of legislators to outlaw open and honest marketing and promotion. If that were true, then any consumer offer to incentivise purchase would be illegal. The legislation is designed to tackle the abuse of power by procurement employees and to promote a level playing field for general trade. Provided any incentive is presented as part of a marketing initiative with the results freely available to those who participate and, indeed, the shareholders of the business, it's just another way to promote business, like advertising.

7.9 Incentive Scheme Examples

Here's an example. An automotive manufacturer is launching a new model and wants to encourage its supporting dealers to build up stock of the product and actively promote it to existing and new customers. The incentive needs to be substantial, eye-catching, and aspirational enough to get the attention, both of the owners of the automotive franchise and of the franchise employees. A package of non-cash incentives may also be put together, including retail vouchers for salespeople and an all-expenses-paid travel trip to Monaco, for the top performers and their partners. There is an incentive website, complete with rules, qualification periods, and an appeals procedure. At the end of the incentive period, the winners are announced to all participants. Tax, if appropriate, is paid to the revenue collectors. The winners and their partners enjoy the event, hosted by the supplier.

Schemes like these are replicated in most developed economies and in many sectors for marketing purposes. These programmes may well be incentives to improve sales activity, but they are not illegal because they comply with bribery legislation which allows for organisational incentive schemes in the form of promotions and advertising.

Take another example. A cell phone manufacturer is introducing a new product to its independent network of retail outlets. It decides that the product is so good that no incentive is required – the product is in high demand, anyway. Unknown to the manufacturer and, indeed, the retailer, an enterprising sales team manager decides that he will personally fund individual sales of the new product with a set amount per confirmed sale which he will give to the salesman when each sale is confirmed. Such a scheme would be illegal because it has been done in secret, without the knowledge of the provider, the customer, or the retail owner. It is designed to influence the seller to propose the new phone to every customer, whether it is suitable or not.

It is obvious to anyone that a scheme like this has the potential to corrupt both the provider of the incentive and the team member receiving it and will distort any sales of the featured product.

7.10 Bribery and Corruption

When you are running a small enterprise, you are unlikely to be supervised by co-directors or trade bodies every day of the week. It is up to you to work out how to best run your business. It can be easy to slip into dubious trade practices under the guise of promoting your business. If this becomes systemic and 'the way things are done around here', you can quite rightly be deemed corrupt.

Here is an example of systematic corruption. Every year, a large manufacturer invites key suppliers to 'a day at the races', including partners, to cement relationships with the network of distributors. One year, the manufacturer decides that invitations to this annual event will now be made by voicemail only and will require the supplier, for the first time, to confirm a specific amount of goods/services to be confirmed in writing, under contract, before an invitation can be sent out. This is clearly in breach of corruption laws which outlaw personal benefit for some future commercial, organisational gain which is undocumented and undeclared. Lack of transparency is the test.

Another example. A local government employee is tasked with choosing an external supplier to provide security arrangements for a large public event involving thousands of potential visitors from the general public. One of the suppliers submits its formal tender as part of the due process. But he then follows up this proposal with a voice call to the employee, who happens to be the chair of the deciding committee, inviting her to attend a similar event they are running in Paris, with partner, with two nights in a luxury hotel, plus dining expenses, 'to see how they do things'.

At one level, this is simply a supplier attempting to demonstrate that they can do the job. However, the inappropriate expense of a foreign travel trip, with partner, to experience the so-called demonstration would contravene most bribery laws, as it can be seen as an attempt to influence a public official in their impartial deliberation as to the most appropriate supplier.

7.11 A Clear Breach of Transparency

Once, many years ago, I ran a hospitality company, charging fees to corporate clients who wanted incentive winners' groups taken overseas. One year, the new marketing director of this long-established client informed me that this year's event would be in Australia. I costed out the project and presented the budget. He asked to have a private meeting about the event a few days later. I assumed it was to do with the fees or some other commercial issue.

He explained that his daughter was getting married in Australia at around the same date span as his corporate event. He would very much like to host a select group of 20 family members to attend. Could I, therefore, rework the budget to include this wedding group, without the knowledge of the client company? All I would have to do, he proposed, was to divide the additional cost by the number of corporate employees attending the event and resubmit the slightly higher per head budget so as to include the cost of the wedding guests.

When you are running your own business, there is a temptation to be as accommodating as possible to clients, especially if they have had a relationship with your business for many years. I had to reply, saying it would not be possible for me to 'hide' the extra costs within the proposal as it would make us uncompetitive within the tendering process, so the answer was no.

In reality, I felt this was not the way I wanted to conduct my business. If we had to 'buy' new clients in this way, we would not have a sustainable model for growing the business in the future. Quite apart from that, it left a nasty taste. I was being asked to enter into a corrupt relationship when I genuinely thought our services were as good as any. We did not see a need for any 'off budget' padding to get the contract.

We failed to confirm the business, which then went to our direct competitor. No reason was given. But you can guess that the new supplier funded the wedding trip. The corporate event (with no mention of the wedding party) was duly written up in the main national trading magazine at that time. No doubt the competitor supplier got some new enquiries as a result. We never worked for that client again.

7.12 Finance and Sales: Two Areas to Watch Regarding Corruption

Statistically, finance and sales are the two areas of your business most likely to be influenced by corrupt ways of doing things.

Finance deals with much larger amounts of money every day than would be considered normal in any household budget. The point about such management of funds is that just a small percentage of any cost can be a significant gain if it goes into the hands of an individual. In the overall scheme of things, the amounts may be so small that most business owners would not notice. But financial auditors do. That's what they are paid to look for.

There are numerous examples of side payments to finance executives for confirming purchases of apparently 'boring' items, such as stationery or insurances. It is not unusual to discover that payments to trusted suppliers over many years have been inflated to cover a 'commission' to someone in the procurement system, unknown to the owner.

But because the amounts were so small, no one bothered to check. It goes without saying that financial team members need to be chosen on the basis of their honesty as well as their ability. You should be able to rely on your financial people to bring to your attention anything out of the ordinary. They are dealing with the numbers all the time, so they will be the first to spot if one of the numbers does not look right. Making numbers add up is what they do for a living, and any anomalies are easy for them to spot.

The management of petty cash and out-of-pocket expenses requires particular attention as it is relatively easy to inflate cash expenses for out-of-pocket expenses and round them up annually, under the guise of 'not worth bothering with' in terms of accuracy. As for any other process in your business, you need a written system for claiming cash expenses and an easy-to-follow trail for receipts. It should all add up correctly.

7.13 Sales Expenses Need to Be Reviewed Regularly

Sales is a notorious area for corruption. Most salespeople work unaccompanied and tend to incur quite substantial travel and hospitality costs as they go about their business. Because they are largely unsupervised, you need robust systems to deal with any expenses which are paid out on behalf of the business.

The main issue, as with bribery, is transparency. You may never dream of spending, say, 500 on an evening out with friends. But sometimes in business, it has to be done in the pursuit of a better relationship. As long as you have the receipts and you can discuss the results of such largesse, all well and good. You may even decide, as a business, that such expenditure is not worth it and discourage salespeople being drawn into offering hospitality by simply arranging meetings mid-morning or mid-afternoon, for example.

The problem comes when the expense claim does not match the documentation. Or the description of the cost is so vague that you start to wonder what was actually spent and where the benefit went. I had one incidence where amounts of 200 and 300 were being submitted regularly in connection with one specific client from a shopping outlet which I knew was not a hotel or a restaurant. One of my financial staff pointed out it was a shoe shop. After further investigation, it turned out the salesman was buying high-end shoes for a lady client as 'gifts' in return for securing contracts on a regular basis with that client.

7.14 Corruption as a Way of Life

It is easy to slide into unacceptable business behaviours under the guise of 'promoting' the organisation. But such practices are now firmly on the legal agenda, with penalties for individual employees for the first time who transgress the law. In some jurisdictions, custodial sentences may be imposed on both the team member and the owner/manager of the business that benefits.

7.15 Keep Your Business Clean

Keeping things clean and honest has another reward over and above just feeling good about yourself. Past or looming court cases will need to be declared should you wish to sell the business and will be covered in the prospective buyer's 'warranties'. A good accountant will also be able to spot any discretional payments made to clients which do not form part of formal contracts. In addition, unusual hospitality costs are simple to highlight when doing a financial audit. They will need to be explained to a purchaser at some stage. They do not stay hidden forever.

Any prospective buyer will be looking for any skeletons in your cupboard before they put serious money on the table. Evidence of sharp practices or unusual payments will come out. Your financial dealings need to be open and honest, for your own sake, when you come to sell the business, not to mention the ethical aspects.

7.16 Ready for Sale?

In the next chapter, I deal with what some people would describe as the whole point of building up any business: *selling it*. Most small business owners have probably toiled away at their business for many years, taking fewer holidays than most and riding the worry and stress of any inevitable economic downturns. They will have benefited from the good times too, of course.

When you come to sell the business, it is often for much more money than you have ever had in your life. In effect, it becomes an investment pot for the future or your retirement fund. Keeping the books clean is simply another part of having something valuable to sell when the time comes. Clean businesses sell for more money than those with something to hide.

KEY LEARNINGS
- It is no longer legally acceptable to turn a blind eye to gifts and inducements in order to win business contracts.
- Gifts to employees and suppliers need to be appropriate and reasonable but, above all, transparent.

- To protect yourself against a malicious claim, keep an internal record of any hospitality given or received, as this is the basis of a successful defence in law.
- Formal incentive schemes can still be a valuable promotional tool in growing your business, but you must be open and honest about the rewards on offer.
- Offering inducements secretly and based on some personal gain in return for a future contract is illegal.
- By keeping your business clean and above board, you make it more sellable when the time comes.

Chapter 8

The Endgame: Selling Your Business

When I bought into my first business, it never occurred to me to value it or have a plan to exit. I was too busy getting customers, recruiting the right team, and making sure I could deliver what I promised. In truth, it was not until the main shareholder and my business partner raised the point that he was thinking of retiring that I even considered the true value of the business I owned.

In hindsight, this was a mistake. As I had no idea what it was worth and had no plan to sell it, I simply kept trading, always hoping to do better than the year before in terms of sales. I never really thought about annual profits, the growth pattern, or getting the business in good shape for sale. As I had no plan apart from some vague idea of growth, my main preoccupation was whether we could pay enough people to service the work we had coming in.

Inevitably, profits were committed to new people or equipment long before the new financial year arrived. The result was that every coming year was already spoken for in terms of cash. Taking profits as dividends was never on the agenda.

                    DOI: 10.4324/9781003532118-9

It was all about how many more sales we could confirm to cover our costs for the following year.

My business partner's impending retirement triggered a completely new approach for me in how to run a business. In fact, all businesses should be started with the endgame in sight. As I said in the 'Introduction', if you don't know where you are going, how do you know when you have arrived?

8.1 Valuing the Business

In the run-up to selling my first business, I came across commercial lawyers and accountants for the first time. They were not the people you would go to for advice about your will, employment law, or the end-of-year tax accounting. To be more accurate, they were acquisition lawyers and dealmakers with a strong financial and commercial background.

The first thing I learned was how to value a business. In short, a buyer will assess your business on its capacity to earn regular, annual profits. Depending on your market, this is then multiplied by a factor – let's call it ×5 or ×10, which represents the number of years the new owner could hope to repeat what you have done without changing very much.

Prospective sellers often ask how you arrive at the 'multiple'. It's often an average of what profits recently sold businesses in the same sector are selling at. This number is probably a function of the average annual profits of the business for the previous three, four, or five years, or whatever is normal for that sector. Any good corporate accountant would know.

If you don't know, the general rule of thumb is that trading businesses – those who simply buy goods in and sell them on at a profit – tend to be based on ×3. This would depend on how many long-term contracts they have, as this determines the multiple of profits. If they have a large sales turnover, the multiple for a 'broking' business could be ×5 or even higher.

Knowledge businesses, such as software creators, unique manufacturers, or indeed, publishers, can command ×10 or more. The principle is that the more difficult it is to recreate the business from scratch, the higher the multiple. It also depends on the strength of their repeat customer database, as this will be the basis of their entire business plan for the year. If it is hard to replicate or acquire, it will attract a bigger multiple.

What if you are not happy with the valuation, perhaps because you were hoping to have more to retire with? If you recognise early on that you are in a transactional business – buy stuff in, sell it on – you can increase the worth of your business by adding 'services', whatever they may be. Usually, it is a paid-for consultancy or an advice arm for which you can charge by the hour. Over the years, this type of add-on service often overshadows the product element in terms of fee income. By the time it is mature, you have a business that is very difficult for competitors to copy, and therefore worth more.

A typical enhancement to any business could be a consumer or trade app which enables customers to use your products and services away from a fixed location. It invariably pushes the buyers into your most popular items and covers a lot more marketing ground than you or your salespeople could do in any given week. This would add real value to your business and make it worth more to a potential buyer.

8.2 Management Accounts Are Essential

So the value of a business is normally made on the average of the last three years' filed accounts. Selling a business after one year of spectacular profits will not cut much ice with most serious buyers. They will probably want to see how you are doing right now. This means being able to show how you are trading, month by month and quarter by quarter. If history shows you have been steadily growing, even better. In other words, what are your management accounts looking like?

Most small businesses do not do management accounts. Big mistake. You should always have a fully rounded picture of all aspects of the business – and this includes regular costs and the trend in sales. It makes it easier to manage and easier to sell on if you know what your end-year profits are going to be.

They don't have to show changes every month if your volumes are small, as nothing much will have changed in four weeks. But the minimum period needs to be quarterly. If you only assess your business performance objectively every year, it will be a long time before you discover things you could improve or stop doing.

8.3 Review Your Business across Many Areas

The value of regular management accounts is that you review where you are across 20–30 headings. It is easy to spot any changes or trends when you do this. This makes it simple to make changes or question costs before it is too late to change the outcome. This applies equally to staff expenses as it does to stationery costs. The very fact that you are looking at the category means you are thinking about them, and taking action, if they are not what you were expecting.

Getting back to a fair valuation, if you make on average, say, 250,000 a year after all costs have been counted, including government or state taxes on profits, and your business can comfortably deliver five more years of similar profits, then the valuation would be in the region of 1.25m.

Most buyers and their commercial lawyers would then start to negotiate on how likely your profits will be stable for the next five years. They will begin to chip away at factors such as how loyal your customers are, whether your key staff will stay after the sale, and how good the market is for your product or service. As all these factors are in the future, no one knows for sure. So the more recorded information from the past you can supply, the more able you will be to support your asking price.

Inevitably, you will have a bad year. This may be due to the economy, new legislation, or even a pandemic. But keep calm. Everyone in your sector will have been affected in the same way. Showing a poor year of results only helps your argument that the business is well-run and that you have things under control. Knowing you are going to make a loss is as important as predicting a profit. In both cases, you are in control.

In the final analysis, the price is what the buyer is prepared to pay to get it. But it helps if you have factual reasons that the price is justified, even if the numbers are not always as good as you would have wanted.

8.4 Tracking the Numbers

The main fact about your business the buyer would like to know is what profits it makes, as certified by a financial professional. The biggest drag on profits is normally staff costs. It therefore makes sense to think from the beginning about remuneration. Are your people paid 'the going rate', or are they leaving for better pay elsewhere? Get in step with your local market and pay good employees what they can get elsewhere or add benefits to compensate. The additional cost is much less than constantly recruiting new people and then having to train them.

You may wish to pay your people for a great year through a bonus or a big salary increase. But be mindful of how it looks on the bottom line for that year. A buyer will have forgotten that you paid out a big bonus in that year and will concentrate on the drop in profits. Bonuses could be spread over two fiscal years, for example, to remove the jump in costs.

8.5 Keep Exceptional Costs to a Minimum

When it comes to being attractive to a buyer, the less exceptional costs you have in the previous or, indeed, coming years, the easier it will be to sell the business on. It's not a good look to the buyer if your place of work is badly maintained or your people are angry about low pay rates or some other human resources issue. These are typical factors which the purchaser's lawyers will use to drive the price down in the final negotiations.

If you do have to upgrade your IT services or take on a new team of people to stay competitive, then make sure the buyer knows this and appreciates how you have taken a hit to improve the business in the long term.

8.6 Management Accounts Mean the Business Is Being Well-Managed

Nothing could be more harmful to the business than failing to keep a track of what the numbers are doing. But it's not the numbers themselves which are important; it's what they represent. Each line of your management accounts forces you to consider whether you are on target or way off target. If the numbers are not looking good, there is clearly something wrong. Either your original target was completely wrong or something is not happening the way you thought it would.

8.7 Who Might Buy Your Business?

It's exciting to think that anyone in the market could find your small business a useful addition to their activities. Your mind races with the potential valuations you might attract, if only you could find the right buyers. There are several business brokers who would be happy to charge you a fee to mail their database of, say, 10,000 'active investors'. However, the chances are very small that they can match you up with a suitable buyer. By definition, you are a small business with customers mainly in your local or national market.

It's probably not going to be international.

Large corporations usually have a defined strategy for acquisitions and will have specific criteria which they will apply when seeking out a new business to own. It may be that they will not start discussions with any entity below a certain size, such as, say, 10m in sales or 1m in regular annual profits.

It may be that you have a very niche product or service that would fit neatly into their family of offerings. So there are exceptions. Software solutions is one such area of expertise. But as a rule, the cost of lawyers' fees and accountancy expenses means it is not cost-effective for them to acquire a small business.

This is particularly true if the parent acquiring organisation is in another country. Language barriers, misinterpretation of accounting terminology, and delays due to the key people not being in the same country – all these facts get in the way of momentum when trying to sell a business. Before you know it, a year has gone by and it seems you are no further forward in achieving your aims. Meanwhile, you are not getting any younger, and nor are they.

8.8 Someone You Know?

The eventual buyer of your business is more likely to be an organisation you already know, probably a competitor. This makes things hard because you don't want to give away your key customer list or your margins – the process whereby you make profits – only to find they do not buy. A straightforward NDA (non-disclosure agreement) with good commercial lawyers will ensure you will not be disadvantaged by sharing your numbers.

The advantages of selling to a direct or indirect competitor are many. They know your industry; they know how to make money in your sector. You will not need to explain any specific industry issues, as you would with a buyer from another sector. It may be that they even know you very well as a personality. That makes it easier to have detailed discussions about any queries they may have regarding your financial projections.

This is important as the price is largely determined by how much they believe your assessment of future profits. If you are projecting, say, a 10% growth rate and your sector is struggling to achieve 2%, you will need to have a very good reason that your business will be the exception.

It's possible that a broker will find you a completely left-field buyer you had never considered before. It could be an individual entrepreneur or a supplier to the same type of customer as you.

Such prospects are good to nurture, even if you are talking to a known competitor. It makes a lot of sense to ensure other interested parties know they are in competition, both in terms of the eventual deal and the urgency with which a deal is being done. There is nothing worse than a single buyer who is querying every number you put on the table, happy in the knowledge that you have no one else lined up to take their place if they delay or pull out of the deal.

8.9 Offers from VCs

One note of caution: it may be that you are approached by a VC (venture capitalist) if you are big enough or a broker for a VC. In essence, they agree to buy a majority stake in your business and you 'earn' the balance of the cash through future business performance, typically over the following three to five years. This is all fine if you are planning to carry on as before. But your new board will possibly be less forgiving than your current team when it comes to profits and performance. If your plan is to sell up and do something else, including retire, a VC will prove to be very irritating and will question every move you make.

8.10 Deal Management Can Be Frustrating

The need for confidentiality on both the buyer and seller sides will mean that you, as owner, will take the brunt of the work regarding the documentation and the speed of decision-making. However well you trust your employed team, you can ill afford to involve them in the early stages as they will be fearful of their own positions post-deal. There may come a time when you wish to involve the key people to ensure they support what you are doing; otherwise, they may try to scupper the deal by being obstructive. One way is to offer cash payments for a successful completion, or even share options in the new organisation, if they don't already have them in the current business.

At the very least, your main financial person will need to be in the picture, as they will be preparing most of the numbers which prospective buyers will want to examine in detail. Most financial employees are, by nature, careful about what they say to outsiders. This is rarely a risk.

Clearly, you will need a lawyer and a financial specialist to help you through the mountains of paperwork. But in the final analysis, it is you who will have to weigh up all the 50/50 decisions which will need to be made during negotiations. This can be tiring and, ultimately, a lonely experience, which is where your psychological resilience comes in (see Chapter 1).

Be prepared to keep things under your hat for many months as the wheels grind slowly when professionals are involved. It is also likely that you will be asked questions or be required to provide specific detail which you don't normally have to hand, such as what percentage of the business is reliant on certain key clients. Or how many days on average are your invoices settled within.

The average time for a successful small business sale is 6–9 months. Often, it will be longer, depending on market conditions or the unpredictability of acquiring new clients. In one instance, I had to postpone a major business sale because one of our three major clients was coming up to contract renewal and buyers would not make a bid until this issue was settled.

8.11 Creating Documentation for Purchasers

Whether you know the buyer or you decide to see what the wider market may offer, you will need a document to attract initial interest. It is sensible not to rely on one potential buyer for your sale. You could waste many months talking to your favourite prospect only to discover they do not have the resources right now to transact the deal, however enthusiastic they may have been at the outset. In any case, it makes commercial sense to have more than one offer, as the buyer will be tempted to offer low if they know they are the only prospect you are talking to.

8.12 Two-Stage Approach: *Overview* and *Prospectus*

If you are contacting a widely dispersed database of prospects, you need to be revealing as much detail as possible to attract serious buyers, but not so much that a potential competitor can guess who you are and cause all kinds of damage amongst your current customers.

The best approach is to create a short *overview* of the business, say, 2–3 pages, outlining what you are selling, the reason for the sale, and some statistical data to show a growing business in a growing sector through bar charts or graphs. You can then add an NDA (non-disclosure agreement), which obliges the prospect to keep subsequent information about the sale confidential and be legally binding, if breached. This should deter any prospects who are simply fishing for market information about your business to attack your clients or steal market ideas.

Once the NDA is signed and received back, you can then afford to issue a more detailed summary of your business, including such information as a list of major clients, financial information for the last three years, and possibly, management accounts for the current year. It will include forecasts for the current year and beyond, as this is exactly what the buyer is purchasing. It may even go into detail about your key employees and any succession plan you have in mind for a new owner. This is normally known as a prospectus or information memorandum.

8.13 What Type of Response Should You Expect to Get?

Any response to your initial *overview* depends on the quality of the list and how many prospects you market to. If you mail 10,000 prospects with fairly loose criteria as to whom to mail, you will get lots of enquiries. But many of them will be advisers who like to keep track of who is selling and competitor tyre-kickers who are just curious.

As a general rule, I would estimate you need to get to around 25 qualified prospects from the first mailing. I would hope for 10 who will sign and return an NDA. Of these 10, you may be lucky and get 3 or 4 serious purchasers who want to progress things with a meeting.

The 10 who show more than passing interest are worth keeping in contact with. Although they may not turn out to want to make an offer, things may change six months later, in their fortunes or yours. So stay on good email terms. They may become a contender once again at some future date.

8.14 Making Voice Contact

There is no substitute for good, old-fashioned voice calls. You may be mystified that so few people want to know more about your business which you have spent a lifetime nurturing. But we are all lazy when it comes to asking for information. The best sales usually come from a polite follow-up by voice. It's only when you listen to someone that you can get their measure and determine whether they really are a good prospect. By talking to the prospective buyer, you can determine a number of key issues which will indicate whether they are truly in the market to buy.

It's also a good opportunity for the seller to find out if the prospect has the money to buy the business, through cash or an agreed loan. Or are they attempting to acquire the business with its own profits by offering staggered payments over the years depending on performance?

The quicker you can eliminate those who will waste your time, the better. We are all familiar with prospects who ask to be contacted in a month's time. Or say it is not their responsibility and will pass your details on to the relevant person, and then never do. Your broker or, indeed, any competent telesales person will understand this and take on as a key task the job of converting interest into action. Or in this case, an initial meeting.

8.15 The Initial Meeting with a Purchaser

So we now have three or four prospects who are interested enough to meet with you in person. What are they really looking for at this stage? The likelihood is that they want to know if there is any chemistry between the two parties. The negotiation could take many months, and no one wants to commit to a long-running business relationship if you simply cannot get on with each other as people. This type of relationship is prone to falling over at the first sign of dispute, usually over the numbers presented.

If you like the prospect, maybe have mutual interests, or clearly respect each other's business acumen, it is more likely there will be some flexibility over the details of the deal. What was seen at the beginning as a red line which could never be crossed could be traded for some other concession if you actually like each other's approach.

The second element which they could be testing is your honesty. It's important to be truthful and consistent, both in documentation and when you speak to the potential buyer. The figures presented in the *overview* and the *prospectus* should reflect reality insofar as the facts are known. Whenever business owners discuss the business with competitors and clients, they often put a positive spin on everything, even if they know things are not looking good right now. This is natural, as all businesses live or die by their next quarter's sales. Even if the contracts are not there right now, there is always hope that they will come good by the end of the period. In fact, they often do.

But you cannot bluster with a buyer. It is remarkable how often things said on the spur of the moment become written in stone in the buyer's mind. If the numbers are simply not true, it leaves an impression that other things may also not be true. What the buyer's advisers will be looking for are ways to reduce the price because of uncertainty or inaccuracy. Don't give the buyer the opportunity to pay less for your business than what it's worth.

The final grey area which they may want more information about is any undeclared, possibly historic, issues which have not been addressed in the documentation. This can be anything from non-payment of taxes to a key employee who is working their notice but you have not declared it. There really is no point in being evasive, as eventually the lawyers will ask you to sign warranties that declare you know of nothing which could reasonably turn out to be a future liability for the purchased business.

8.16 Legal and Accounting Issues

If the potential buyer sees no red flags once they have met you in person and wants to go further, you will then embark on a roller-coaster ride of emotions as presented by the involvement of specialist lawyers and accountants. This is where the deal makes it over the line or falls flat on its face. It could be a few months or potentially a year or more, depending on what the advisers uncover. The key point is to stay calm, not take things personally, and continue to run the business as if the discussions were not taking place at all. Whatever you do, don't delay improvements or new hires just because you are in discussion. There is a good chance the deal may not go ahead anyway, depending on the nature of your business and the buyer's finances.

Let's talk legal first. The job of your legal adviser is to prevent you from signing up to something which will depress the asking price or allow for monies to be clawed back at some future date if it can be proved you claimed something which was not true. The standard list of warranties – things which you will take legal and cost responsibility for post-sale – usually runs to about a hundred questions or more, if you want to be totally watertight in terms of future liabilities. This process is sometimes known as due diligence and can include anything and everything the buyer does not know about your business. If there is a skeleton in the cupboard, this is how the buyer finds it. And they will – make no mistake about it.

If there is something you know about for sure and you are happy to take the risk as something that will never happen, agree to the warranty. A good example is whether there are any current or pending court cases against the business. This is not something the buyer can easily investigate. By asking for a warranty, they get the comfort that this is not a risk. But if it does turn out to be true, they can be financially compensated.

Clearly, there are some things which are impossible to warrant, such as none of your employees ever being a fraud risk or stealing from the business. No one can guarantee that this will never happen, so you can refuse to grant that warranty. It doesn't mean the deal is off. It simply tests the resolve of the buyer to acquire the business with a bit of risk. In simple terms, the buyer wants you to agree to as many warranties as he can get so he can buy with no future risk. The seller wants to agree to no warranties at all so that he has no future liabilities, especially if the business has been sold. Inevitably, it's a compromise between buyer and seller as to how many warranties you both want to sign up to.

Sometimes the seller will want to ask for compensation if the new buyer is already planning to sell the new business on within a few months and make a huge profit. Nothing wrong with that. It's just business, as they say. But if you suspect the buyer has already lined up a new owner, even before your deal is done, the lawyer should be advising you to put in a clause that claws back some of those additional profits and gives them to you.

You may think this is very odd and hardly ever happens. Not true.

When I sold my first business, negotiations went on well into the early hours, having started at lunchtime. By 3:00 a.m., everyone was ready to call it a day and sign the papers. My lawyer suddenly decided to throw in this 'future profits' clause with a time limit of five years, much to everyone's annoyance, including my own. But everyone was too tired to argue about it. So it went in.

Four and a half years later, I took a call from the same lawyer who said the people who had bought my business wanted to sell it on to a larger concern, and could I consent to it? I had forgotten all about the clause in question. The bigger deal could not go ahead financially unless I gave my approval in return for the very large sum agreed in the original sale. Of course I said yes, for doing nothing other than sign my name.

The thing to remember about legal issues is that some just need to be agreed because it's normal business practice. Others are simply a way for the buyer to load the seller with future obligations and so reduce the eventual price. As in all commercial dealings, there comes a point when either side may decide that the obligations are too risky, financially speaking, and they pull out of the contract.

It needs to be said that both sides will have spent so much on independent advice by that stage that neither will want to call a halt to the deal. A last-minute compromise is often reached. The deal goes ahead, and neither party can even remember what the hold-up was all about six months later.

But be prepared for high anxiety and brinkmanship towards the end of the negotiating period. It's nothing personal. It may be just lawyers being lawyers, so let them do what they do best.

8.17 Types of Deal

Many people who have not been through the process of selling their business believe that on deal day, the owner simply walks away with a bag full of cash.

This is certainly one scenario, but it lies at the very edge of the more usual outcomes. In fact, deals to sell your business range from a single cash lump sum on deal day at one extreme to a very small amount on deal day with payments being made over several years until the agreed selling price is paid out from future profits at the other.

Why is there such a discrepancy? It's all about risk, of course. Sometimes it's also about your local country tax regime.

Let's consider paying out the complete sum on deal day. In this unlikely scenario, the buyer is totally confident that what they are paying for is exactly what was offered in the documentation and that they have no need of the owner beyond deal day. There is very little 'comfort' in this arrangement for the buyer should things turn out not as expected. It can happen with smaller deals, where the legal and financial costs of hedging your bets are simply not worth the financial benefit.

The more normal deal day situation is that a large proportion of the agreed price is paid over, with any balance being due in subsequent years, normally two or three, dependent on whether the profits the seller outlined happen in reality. It may also be that an additional premium would be paid if the profits exceed what the seller projected for the agreed price, after deal day.

A further element may be the requirement for the previous owner to stay involved with the business for a set period to smooth over the transition to the new team. This option can sometimes be completely unacceptable to the seller, as they tend to mentally prepare themselves to 'retire' from the business completely. But in most circumstances, it is an opportunity for the owner perhaps to work for less days per year but still be earning remuneration while looking for other business opportunities.

The new owners may find the transition easier than expected and 'release' the former owner from their paid obligations in return for a personal exit fee. If you judge that this is more likely to happen than not, you could get your lawyer to write in a fixed fee to the agreement, whether you stay for the full term or not.

When things go wrong, they can go badly wrong. It sometimes happens that the former owner was so instrumental in the success of the business that once they have gone, customer relationships fall away and profits reduce or even collapse in the following financial periods. In such cases, the buyer may sue the former owner for misrepresentation and try to claw back some of the purchase price. This is notoriously difficult to achieve through the legal system, following the 'caveat emptor' ('let the buyer beware') principle.

It is expected that the buyer would have done enough due diligence pre-deal to know whether a collapse in sales would be likely and so would have reduced the price or not done the deal at all.

8.18 Telling the Team

If you have been able to keep the details of the deal confidential to just a few key employees, the announcement of a new owner will have a profound effect on your existing team. Some could be delighted, as they may see career opportunities with a new owner. Others may be fearful of their continued employment, especially if they consider themselves to be in duplicated roles, such as in finance, HR, or marketing.

Your obligation to the new owner is to try to smooth over any negatives in return for the cash consideration they will have just paid or are promising to pay.

In general, a personal address by you to the team explaining the reasons for the sale and an introduction to the new executive team may be appropriate. In other cases, the new owner may wish to have a clean break and ask you to leave immediately once the money is handed over.

8.19 Managing Your Exit

Whichever method is chosen, it is up to the new owner to decide how to handle things, as the business is now in their possession. You may deeply disagree with the way they want the transition to happen, but you have the compensation of knowing that you have successfully realised a considerable asset. It is no longer your role to 'manage' the business, either strategically or in detail. This will be very hard for the former owner if they have been intimately involved in the details of the business for many years. But the reality is that the business is now under new management, and you must give way to how the new owners want to do things.

Ideally, the new owner will allow you to say your goodbyes personally to the team, stay on in some kind of consultancy role, and gradually transition your way out of the business.

Leaving the business for good is often the hardest part of any entrepreneur's journey. Relationships may have been built up over many years, and you create strong bonds of joint working which often spill over into personal lives. It's hard to step back and let someone else take over when you know so much about how best to get things done. It's even harder if the new owner insists you 'book an appointment' to visit the offices in the future so they can keep a track on you as a visitor.

You need to be ever mindful that having new bosses for your old team may create some resistance from them. No one likes change. You may be pulled unwittingly into intervening with the new owners about new ways of working by disgruntled employees. This is to be resisted. It's not your business anymore. Your intervention, formally or informally, may be perceived as a breach of contract if you are under some kind of financial arrangement.

In almost all cases, it is best to withdraw gracefully and not get involved in any disputes or disagreements. You have done your bit over the years and got your reward. It's now up to the new owners to make what they can out of what they have bought.

8.20 How Did It Go?

When the dust has settled on the deal and you are either working towards your exit or have actually left the business, it's natural to think back and consider how you did. Did it go as expected? Could you have done things better? If you started again, what would you improve on? In the final chapter, we will explore the final reckoning and hopefully find ways to close the book on a job well done.

KEY LEARNINGS

- Keep the endgame in sight. What would you be happy to sell for?
- Get the business valued by a professional on a regular basis.
- Get into the habit of doing regular management accounts, however basic.
- Appoint legal and financial people who specialise in business sales.
- Adopt the two-stage approach: overview and prospectus/information memorandum.
- Every deal is different; there are no givens to a successful business sale.
- Think about how the sale news will affect the team, and plan accordingly.
- Manage your exit from the business carefully.
- Be prepared to 'disappear', even if you really like the people and know how things, in your opinion, are best done.

Chapter 9

How Did We Do?

An honest assessment of how things are going or how they went is at the heart of being a successful entrepreneur. Contrary to how entrepreneurs are perceived by the wider world, it's not always about the money. Even entrepreneurs have real lives, too, and can be very emotional about business issues. But I use the words 'How did WE do?' because all businesses are a team effort, even though as owner you may well be able to monetise your efforts better than other team members.

9.1 But Let's Start with the Money

As a small business owner, the buck stops with you in terms of people's jobs and well-being at work. You need to make a profit. So keeping track of the money is a vital part of long-term success. It doesn't have to be a fortune. But it would be good to know that there are some rewards for the responsibility you take on as an owner. Otherwise, you may as well play it safe, work for a large organisation or the government,

DOI: 10.4324/9781003532118-10

and clock out at the end of the week with your weekends worry-free.

9.2 What Would I Have Earned in a Lifetime's Work?

It all depends on where you work, what sector you are in, and for how long, of course. But let's assume you start work at age 21 after college or university and work until you are 65. That's 44 years. As a salaried employee, your income will increase for a certain amount of time, then level off.

Looking at my early career, I can see that my income rose from around 20,000 to 40,000 for the first ten years. If I had remained working for someone else, I could see myself reaching, say, VP level by retirement at 65, so another 34 years. I could have been on, say, 100,000 for the last five years. If I do the calculations, I will have earned about 3 million, but spent most of it.

Not bad. But of course, we all have expenses, and I can safely say in all my employed years I rarely had more than 5% of take-home pay left at the end of the month. All things considered, that leaves me with 5% of 3m for a lifetime's work. A net total of 150,000. I've probably excluded superannuation savings. There's also my house, which would have grown in value over the years, if the market helped me out. But I cannot cash it in because I need somewhere to live, after all.

9.3 A Good Net Result after 44 Years

So as an employee, I would have come out of the other end of 44 years of business life with a relatively modest positive sum.

About the only upside is that I would not have been solely responsible for the welfare of other people, and you could argue that the working week is less financially stressful for an individual than an owner, in theory. Your weekends are your own, unless you make it to the C-suite.

That said, senior executives are constantly under pressure to manage people well and deliver the numbers, so it is not all plain-sailing. The higher you go up, the more likely your job would be at risk. You would have little control over that situation. You may lose your job through mergers or acquisitions. Or maybe the market has moved on for your specific skill. You may find yourself having to seek work overseas simply to remain in position on current benefits or share options.

9.4 What Did I Earn in a Lifetime's 'Entrepreneurship'?

As it took me ten years to stumble into owning a business, my earnings up to age 31 were just enough to cover my outgoings for a growing family of three children and a wife who did not have the time for full-time employment.

Over the 34 years of entrepreneurial ownership, I accumulated around 4.5m *over and above* annual salaries and benefits. These payments were directly into my bank account after each transaction. You never get something for nothing, so you need to subtract my share of the buying costs on each deal. But that would be no more than 350,000 in total. Legal and accounting costs were paid for by the organisations I owned or partly owned. More importantly, as the boss, I could set my remuneration at whatever figure was reasonable, bearing in mind local taxation rules and the going rate for the top job in each business. In broad terms, you can assume that my monthly outgoings were taken care of by my remuneration package, with a good amount spare each month.

I always paid myself the going rate and was the most highly paid employee in my businesses. In my mind, paying yourself nothing to show profits in the business is self-defeating, as a potential buyer would always need to pay for your replacement. If you pay yourself nothing, the acquirer will just add on a market-rate salary to the costs before they make an offer for your business. So you are no better off being mean to yourself.

9.5 The Result, Financially?

I don't consider myself to have been a great innovator, public speaker, or marketer during my career. I simply followed the logic of running businesses positively and kept a wary eye on the cash. Was it all worth the risk?

All in all, I made 4m, over and above remuneration, in my career. If I compare that result with what I would probably have netted as a corporate employee, that would have been, say, 150,000. Being an entrepreneur has brought me 27 times more cash to retire with than having had an employed position. Financially, for me, it has been a no-brainer.

9.6 But How about Other Measures?

Having dealt with the money side of owning and running a business, there are other ways to measure whether I did well or not.

They fall into the following categories:

■ Control over my working life
■ Ability to make substantial investments

- Staying local
- Job satisfaction
- Leaving something behind for others

9.7 Control over My Working Life

Some experts say that control over your own life reduces stress and leads to a more enjoyable experience. The benefits of being employed, psychologically, are much overrated. Admittedly, there is an underlying feeling of support with a regular pay cheque coming in. You know you can pay your bills at the end of the month and perhaps save a little for the future.

But this illusion of security only lasts if your employer makes no changes or mistakes. With a long-established employer in former times in a reputable business, you might survive for decades. With the coming of the Internet, many so-called traditional businesses have been challenged to do things more efficiently than ever before. Experts now point to a trading cycle of just three years before the business plan has to be rewritten to accommodate market changes. It used to be ten years, reducing to five years.

9.8 No Employed Job Is Safe

The implication for employed workers is that no job is 'safe' for more than three years. That means you should be looking around for other employment at the start of your third year, just in case. For many people, the promise of a new career in a new setting lasts no longer than this initial three-year period. The likelihood is that you will not find another work role nearby and will have to relocate or work away during the week. This is not something that you could describe as being in control of your life.

As an entrepreneur, you largely dictate your working life as you are in charge. Naturally, you can decide to take on new tasks or spend time away from home, if you think the development of the business merits it. The point is, that's your decision to take. It will not be something imposed from above or dictated by market circumstances.

9.9 Ability to Make Substantial Investments

At the end of the accounting year, as owner, you will be entitled to receive all the profits of the business, in addition to your remuneration, whatever you decide that is.

The first decision you can make is to keep the money within the legal framework of the business. This allows you to do some income tax planning, something you would not be able to do as an employed person. Depending on your tax regime, you could pay yourself mostly in dividends, which would attract a lower rate of tax than simply taking a salary.

If you still have some cash left over, you might decide to retain the cash in the business account to be ready for any unexpected costs of trading or perhaps a known expense for the following financial year. Some businesses are cash-positive, in that they are able to collect revenue before it is spent. But not many. Most small enterprises have to pay for supplier services many months before they get paid by their clients. So keeping money aside in anticipation of debts is always a good idea.

But what do you do if you have done all these calculations and there is still a substantial amount of money left over at the end of the year? You use it to grow the business through buying new or enhanced production equipment. Or you use it as a fund to acquire another or, indeed, several businesses. Or you could invest it in stocks.

All the businesses I set up from scratch were done with accumulated funds from previous businesses, so the cost of funding them was zero. The first successful business provided enough spare cash to fund the next one, and so on. If a business made a loss, then the only debt I had was to myself.

I kept score of what I had invested and what came out the other end in terms of surplus. Sometimes, when you add in all the buying and selling fees of professionals, I barely broke even on those investments. But it made the whole business group bigger, and therefore more attractive to potential buyers. If I had simply left the money in the bank, it would certainly have grown by a small amount, depending on interest rates. But with no chance of large gains. Unless you take risks, there can be no reward.

9.10 Staying Local

Owning your own business gives you the opportunity to work in a location that suits you. For many people, putting down roots and bringing up a family in one place provide great stability for you, your family, and your ever-growing business network. I have seen the difference having grown up in over a dozen separate places, always changing schools, never really getting settled anywhere as part of a community. Being in one place provides a less-stressful homelife. Other members of the family can get on with their lives without worrying if they will need to uproot themselves at any given moment because of work decisions taken by other people.

Since owning my own business in my early 30s, I have lived in the same area where I now live in my 60s. The children grew up here, and one of them even lives in the same village with her children. As an employed person, I fully realise that you have to chase the money or the promotion to make the most of your talents. Sometimes you need to up sticks and move on because your employer got it wrong, commercially speaking.

But being your own boss means you can decide whether to move away, perhaps even to a different country, to make the best of things, rather than be forced to do it because of someone else's business strategy.

9.11 Job Satisfaction

Feeling good about what you do and being successful at it are both satisfying and psychologically rewarding. Of the many motivational studies I have come across over the years, a piece by Henry Murray (1938) about *20 basic human needs* stood out. He emphasised the motivational power to the individual of the need to 'exercise personal skills or talents'. Naturally, many people get similar levels of satisfaction from being valued as an employed team member or in a profession. But they rarely have the added bonus of being in control of your own financial rewards as you do when you are a business owner.

9.12 Legacy, Leaving Something behind for Others

One of the many benefits of being an entrepreneur is the opportunity to leave a legacy behind when you are no longer the head of a business. Politicians, actors, and artists all leave something behind when they leave the public stage – some worthwhile, some not so impressive. I have taken great personal satisfaction in leaving businesses behind that have grown, expanded, and done worthwhile work and projects. Even though the names and ownerships may have changed, I know that unless I had started them all those years ago, they would not now have still been around, doing good work, and provided stimulating work for people. It's a legacy I'm proud to have been part of. It would never have happened had I not, at some stage in my 30s, taken a risk and become an entrepreneur.

9.13 The Reckoning

Owners like to keep score. For those who like to see the numbers, I have listed in what follows an approximate recollection of the financial side of my businesses over the years. Nothing has been straightforward. You will see that things have been up and down.

My biggest success was paying 50,000 for a half share in a business that netted me 2.7m some nine years later. I also bought an app software business for 275,000 and sold it for just 310,000. I also took a good salary from it as well, so it was not as marginal as that looks.

I started up two businesses from scratch, so technically there was no investment and no initial cost. The eventual sale price was all gain.

None of the businesses I bought and sold were the same in terms of initial investment and final outcome. Being a successful entrepreneur is really a question of working with the cards you are dealt and making the best of the hand you find yourself with.

9.14 Persistence Is the Key

If there is one overriding lesson to pass on to would-be entrepreneurs, it is this: *keeping on*. Keeping on is the characteristic trait of many successful business people. The key quality to have is *persistence*. Whether you have the brains or the health or the resources is less important than to keep going. Nothing beats persistence when it comes to achieving results. If you keep making the effort, sooner or later, you will succeed.

Index

Printed in the United States
by Baker & Taylor Publisher Services